DANTES SUBJECT STANDARDIZED TESTS

THIS IS YOUR **PASSBOOK®** FOR ...

INTRODUCTION TO CARPENTRY

NATIONAL LEARNING CORPORATION®
passbooks.com

PASSBOOK® SERIES

THE *PASSBOOK® SERIES* has been created to prepare applicants and candidates for the ultimate academic battlefield – the examination room.

At some time in our lives, each and every one of us may be required to take an examination – for validation, matriculation, admission, qualification, registration, certification, or licensure.

Based on the assumption that every applicant or candidate has met the basic formal educational standards, has taken the required number of courses, and read the necessary texts, the *PASSBOOK® SERIES* furnishes the one special preparation which may assure passing with confidence, instead of failing with insecurity. Examination questions – together with answers – are furnished as the basic vehicle for study so that the mysteries of the examination and its compounding difficulties may be eliminated or diminished by a sure method.

This book is meant to help you pass your examination provided that you qualify and are serious in your objective.

The entire field is reviewed through the huge store of content information which is succinctly presented through a provocative and challenging approach – the question-and-answer method.

A climate of success is established by furnishing the correct answers at the end of each test.

You soon learn to recognize types of questions, forms of questions, and patterns of questioning. You may even begin to anticipate expected outcomes.

You perceive that many questions are repeated or adapted so that you can gain acute insights, which may enable you to score many sure points.

You learn how to confront new questions, or types of questions, and to attack them confidently and work out the correct answers.

You note objectives and emphases, and recognize pitfalls and dangers, so that you may make positive educational adjustments.

Moreover, you are kept fully informed in relation to new concepts, methods, practices, and directions in the field.

You discover that you arre actually taking the examination all the time: you are preparing for the examination by "taking" an examination, not by reading extraneous and/or supererogatory textbooks.

In short, this PASSBOOK®, used directedly, should be an important factor in helping you to pass your test.

NONTRADITIONAL EDUCATION

Students returning to school as adults bring more varied experience to their studies than do the teenagers who begin college shortly after graduating from high school. As a result, there are numerous programs for students with nontraditional learning curves. Hundreds of colleges and universities grant degrees to people who cannot attend classes at a regular campus or have already learned what the college is supposed to teach.

You can earn nontraditional education credits in many ways:
- Passing standardized exams
- Demonstrating knowledge gained through experience
- Completing campus-based coursework, and
- Taking courses off campus

Some methods of assessing learning for credit are objective, such as standardized tests. Others are more subjective, such as a review of life experiences.

With some help from four hypothetical characters – Alice, Vin, Lynette, and Jorge – this article describes nontraditional ways of earning educational credit. It begins by describing programs in which you can earn a high school diploma without spending 4 years in a classroom. The college picture is more complicated, so it is presented in two parts: one on gaining credit for what you know through course work or experience, and a second on college degree programs. The final section lists resources for locating more information.

Earning High School Credit

People who were prevented from finishing high school as teenagers have several options if they want to do so as adults. Some major cities have back-to-school programs that allow adults to attend high school classes with current students. But the more practical alternatives for most adults are to take the General Educational Development (GED) tests or to earn a high school diploma by demonstrating their skills or taking correspondence classes.

Of course, these options do not match the experience of staying in high school and graduating with one's friends. But they are viable alternatives for adult learners committed to meeting and, often, continuing their educational goals.

GED Program

Alice quit high school her sophomore year and took a job to help support herself, her younger brother, and their newly widowed mother. Now an adult, she wants to earn her high school diploma – and then go on to college. Because her job as head cook and her family responsibilities keep her busy during the day, she plans to get a high school equivalency diploma. She will study for, and take, the GED tests. Every year, about half a million adults earn their high school credentials this way. A GED diploma is accepted in lieu of a high school one by more than 90 percent of employers, colleges, and universities, so it is a good choice for someone like Alice.

The GED testing program is sponsored by the American Council on Education and State and local education departments. It consists of examinations in five subject areas: Writing, science, mathematics, social studies, and literature and the arts. The tests also measure skills such as analytical ability, problem solving, reading comprehension, and ability to understand and apply information. Most of the questions are multiple choice; the writing test includes an essay section on a topic of general interest.

Eligibility rules for taking the exams vary, but some states require that you must be at least 18. Tests are given in English, Spanish, and French. In addition to standard print, versions in large print, Braille, and audiocassette are also available. Total time allotted for the tests is 7 1/2 hours.

The GED tests are not easy. About one-fourth of those who complete the exams every year do not pass. Passing scores are established by administering the tests to a sample of graduating high school seniors. The minimum standard score is set so that about one-third of graduating seniors would not pass the tests if they took them.

Because of the difficulty of the tests, people need to prepare themselves to take them. Often, they start by taking the Official GED Practice Tests, usually available through a local adult education center. Centers are listed in your phone book's blue pages under "Adult Education," "Continuing Education," or "GED." Adult education centers also have information about GED preparation classes and self-study materials. Classes are generally arranged to accommodate adults' work schedules. National Learning Corporation publishes several study guides that aim to thoroughly prepare test-takers for the GED.

School districts, colleges, adult education centers, and community organizations have information about GED testing schedules and practice tests. For more information, contact them, your nearest GED testing center, or:

GED Testing Service
One Dupont Circle, NW, Suite 250
Washington, DC 20036-1163
1(800) 62-MY GED (626-9433)
(202) 939-9490

Skills Demonstration

Adults who have acquired high school level skills through experience might be eligible for the National External Diploma Program. This alternative to the GED does not involve any direct instruction. Instead, adults seeking a high school diploma must demonstrate mastery of 65 competencies in 8 general areas: Communication; computation; occupational preparedness; and self, social, consumer, scientific, and technological awareness.

Mastery is shown through the completion of the tasks. For example, a participant could prove competency in computation by measuring a room for carpeting, figuring out the amount of carpet needed, and computing the cost.

Before being accepted for the program, adults undergo an evaluation. Tests taken at one of the program's offices measure reading, writing, and mathematics abilities. A take-home segment includes a self-assessment of current skills, an individual skill evaluation, and an occupational interest and aptitude test.

Adults accepted for the program have weekly meetings with an assessor. At the meeting, the assessor reviews the participant's work from the previous week. If the task has not been completed properly, the assessor explains the mistake. Participants continue to correct their errors until they master each competency. A high school diploma is awarded upon proven mastery of all 65 competencies.

Fourteen States and the District of Columbia now offer the External Diploma Program. For more information, contact:

External Diploma Program
One Dupont Circle, NW, Suite 250
Washington, DC 20036-1193
(202) 939-9475

Correspondence and Distance Study

Vin dropped out of high school during his junior year because his family's frequent moves made it difficult for him to continue his studies. He promised himself at the time he dropped out that he would someday finish the courses needed for his diploma. For people like Vin, who prefer to earn a traditional diploma in a nontraditional way, there are about a dozen accredited courses of study for earning a high school diploma by correspondence, or distance study. The programs are either privately run, affiliated with a university, or administered by a State education department.

Distance study diploma programs have no residency requirements, allowing students to continue their studies from almost any location. Depending on the course of study, students need not be enrolled full time and usually have more flexible schedules for finishing their work. Selection of courses ranges from vo-tech to college prep, and some programs place different emphasis on the types of diplomas offered. University affiliated schools, for example, allow qualified students to take college courses along with their high school ones. Students can then apply the college credits toward a degree at that university or transfer them to another institution.

Taking courses by distance study is often more challenging and time consuming than attending classes, especially for adults who have other obligations. Success depends on each student's motivation. Students usually do reading assignments on their own. Written exercises, which they complete and send to an instructor for grading, supplement their reading material.

A list of some accredited high schools that offer diplomas by distance study is available free from the Distance Education and Training Council, formerly known as the National Home Study Council. Request the "DETC Directory of Accredited Institutions" from:

The Distance Education and Training Council
1601 18th Street, NW.
Washington, DC 20009-2529
(202) 234-5100

Some publications profiling nontraditional college programs include addresses and descriptions of several high school correspondence ones. See the Resources section at the end of this article for more information.

Getting College Credit For What You Know

Adults can receive college credit for prior coursework, by passing examinations, and documenting experiential learning. With help from a college advisor, nontraditional students should assess their skills, establish their educational goals, and determine the number of college credits they might be eligible for.

Even before you meet with a college advisor, you should collect all your school and training records. Then, make a list of all knowledge and abilities acquired through experience, no matter how irrelevant they seem to your chosen field. Next, determine your educational goals: What specific field do you wish to study? What kind of a degree do you want? Finally, determine how your past work fits into the field of study. Later on, you will evaluate educational programs to find one that's right for you.

People who have complex educational or experiential learning histories might want to have their learning evaluated by the Regents Credit Bank. The Credit Bank, operated by Regents College of the University of the State of New York, allows people to consolidate credits earned through college, experience, or other methods. Special assessments are available for Regents College enrollees whose knowledge in a specific field cannot be adequately evaluated by standardized exams. For more information, contact the Regents Credit Bank at:

Regents College
7 Columbia Circle
Albany, NY 12203-5159
(518) 464-8500

Credit For Prior College Coursework

When Lynette was in college during the 1970s, she attended several different schools and took a variety of courses. She did well in some classes and poorly in others. Now that she is a successful business owner and has more focus, Lynette thinks she should forget about her previous coursework and start from scratch. Instead, she should start from where she is.

Lynette should have all her transcripts sent to the colleges or universities of her choice and let an admissions officer determine which classes are applicable toward a degree. A few credits here and there may not seem like much, but they add up. Even if the subjects do not seem relevant to any major, they might be counted as elective credits toward a degree. And comparing the cost of transcripts with the cost of college courses, it makes sense to spend a few dollars per transcript for a chance to save hundreds, and perhaps thousands, of dollars in books and tuition.

Rules for transferring credits apply to all prior coursework at accredited colleges and universities, whether done on campus or off. Courses completed off campus, often called extended learning, include those available to students through independent study and correspondence. Many schools have extended learning programs; Brigham Young University, for example, offers more than 300 courses through its Department of Independent Study. One type of extended learning is distance learning, a form of correspondence study by technological means such as television, video and audio, CD-ROM, electronic mail, and computer tutorials. See the Resources section at the end of this article for more information about publications available from the National University Continuing Education Association.

Any previously earned college credits should be considered for transfer, no matter what the subject or the grade received. Many schools do not accept the transfer of courses graded below a C or ones taken more than a designated number of years ago. Some colleges and universities also have limits on the number of credits that can be transferred and applied toward a degree. But not all do. For example, Thomas Edison State College, New Jersey's State college for adults, accepts the transfer of all 120 hours of credit required for a baccalaureate degree – provided all the credits are transferred from regionally accredited schools, no more than 80 are at the junior college level, and the student's grades overall and in the field of study average out to C.

To assign credit for prior coursework, most schools require original transcripts. This means you must complete a form or send a written, signed request to have your transcripts released directly to a college or university. Once you have chosen the schools you want to apply to, contact the schools you attended before. Find out how much each transcript costs, and ask them to send your transcripts to the ones you are applying to. Write a letter that includes your name (and names used during attendance, if different) and dates of attendance, along with the names and addresses of the schools to which your transcripts should be sent. Include payment and mail to the registrar at the schools you have attended. The registrar's office will process your request and send an official transcript of your coursework to the colleges or universities you have designated.

Credit For Noncollege Courses

Colleges and universities are not the only ones that offer classes. Volunteer organizations and employers often provide formal training worth college credit. The American Council on Education has two programs that assess thousands of specific courses and make recommendations on the amount of college credit they are worth. Colleges and universities accept the recommendations or use them as guidelines.

One program evaluates educational courses sponsored by government agencies, business and industry, labor unions, and professional and voluntary organizations. It is the Program on Noncollegiate Sponsored Instruction (PONSI). Some of the training seminars Alice has participated in covered topics such as food preparation, kitchen safety, and nutrition. Although she has not yet earned her GED, Alice can earn college credit because of her completion of these formal job-training seminars. The number of credits each seminar is worth does not hinge on Alice's current eligibility for college enrollment.

The other program evaluates courses offered by the Army, Navy, Air Force, Marines, Coast Guard, and Department of Defense. It is the Military Evaluations Program. Jorge has never attended college, but the engineering technology classes he completed as part of his military training are worth college credit. And as an Army veteran, Jorge is eligible for a service that takes the evaluations one step further. The Army/American Council on Education Registry Transcript System (AARTS) will provide Jorge with an individualized transcript of American Council on Education credit recommendations for all courses he completed, the military occupational specialties (MOS's) he held, and examinations he passed while in the Army. All Army and National Guard enlisted personnel and veterans who enlisted after October 1981 are eligible for the transcript. Similar services are being considered by the Navy and Marine Corps.

To obtain a free transcript, see your Army Education Center for a 5454R transcript request form. Include your name, Social Security number, basic active service date, and complete address where you want the transcript sent. Mail your request to:

AARTS Operations Center
415 McPherson Ave.
Fort Leavenworth, KS 66027-1373

Recommendations for PONSI are published in *The National Guide to Educational Credit for Training Programs;* military program recommendations are in *The Guide to the Evaluation of Educational Experiences in the Armed Forces.* See the Resources section at the end of this article for more information about these publications.

Former military personnel who took a foreign language course through the Defense Language Institute may request course transcripts by sending their name, Social Security number, course title, duration of the course, and graduation date to:

Commandant, Defense Language Institute
Attn: ATFL-DAA-AR
Transcripts
Presidio of Monterey
Monterey, CA 93944-5006

Not all of Jorge's and Alice's courses have been assessed by the American Council on Education. Training courses that have no Council credit recommendation should still be assessed by an advisor at the schools they want to attend. Course descriptions, class notes, test scores, and other documentation may be helpful for comparing training courses to their college equivalents. An oral examination or other demonstration of competency might also be required.

There is no guarantee you will receive all the credits you are seeking – but you certainly won't if you make no attempt.

Credit By Examination

Standardized tests are the best-known method of receiving college credit without taking courses. These exams are often taken by high school students seeking advanced placement for college, but they are also available to adult learners. Testing programs and colleges and universities offer exams in a number of subjects. Two U.S. Government institutes have foreign language exams for employees that also may be worth college credit.

It is important to understand that receiving a passing score on these exams does not mean you get college credit automatically. Each school determines which test results it will accept, minimum scores required, how scores are converted for credit, and the amount of credit, if any, to be assigned. Most colleges and universities accept the American Council on Education credit recommendations, published every other year in the 250-page *Guide to Educational Credit by Examination*. For more information, contact:

The American Council on Education
Credit by Examination Program
One Dupont Circle, Suite 250
Washington, DC 20036-1193
(202) 939-9434

Testing programs:

You might know some of the five national testing programs by their acronyms or initials: CLEP, ACT PEP: RCE, DANTES, AP, and NOCTI. (The meanings of these initialisms are explained below.) There is some overlap among programs; for example, four of them have introductory accounting exams. Since you will not be awarded credit more than once for a specific subject, you should carefully evaluate each program for the subject exams you wish to take. And before taking an exam, make sure you will be awarded credit by the college or university you plan to attend.

CLEP (College-Level Examination Program), administered by the College Board, is the most widely accepted of the national testing programs; more than 2,800 accredited schools award credit for passing exam scores. Each test covers material taught in basic undergraduate courses. There are five general exams – English composition, humanities, college mathematics, natural sciences, and social sciences and history – and many subject exams. Most exams are entirely multiple-choice, but English composition exams may include an essay section. For more information, contact:

CLEP
P.O. Box 6600
Princeton, NJ 08541-6600
(609) 771-7865

ACT PEP: RCE (American College Testing Proficiency Exam Program: Regents College Examinations) tests are given in 38 subjects within arts and sciences, business, education, and nursing. Each exam is recommended for either lower- or upper-level credit. Exams contain either objective or extended response questions, and are graded according to a standard score, letter grade, or pass/fail. Fees vary, depending on the subject and type of exam. For more information or to request free study guides, contact:

ACT PEP: Regents College Examinations
P.O. Box 4014
Iowa City, IA 52243
(319) 337-1387
(New York State residents must contact Regents College directly.)

DANTES (Defense Activity for Nontraditional Education Support) standardized tests are developed by the Educational Testing Service for the Department of Defense. Originally administered only to military personnel, the exams have been available to the public since 1983. About 50 subject tests cover business, mathematics, social science, physical science, humanities, foreign languages, and applied technology. Most of the tests consist entirely of multiple-choice questions. Schools determine their own administering fees and testing schedules. For more information or to request free study sheets, contact:

DANTES Program Office
Mail Stop 31-X
Educational Testing Service
Princeton, NJ 08541
1(800) 257-9484

The AP (Advanced Placement) Program is a cooperative effort between secondary schools and colleges and universities. AP exams are developed each year by committees of college and high school faculty appointed by the College Board and assisted by consultants from the Educational Testing Service. Subjects include arts and languages, natural sciences, computer science, social sciences, history, and mathematics. Most tests are 2 or 3 hours long and include both multiple-choice and essay questions. AP courses are available to help students prepare for exams, which are offered in the spring. For more information about the Advanced Placement Program, contact:

Advanced Placement Services
P.O. Box 6671
Princeton, NJ 08541-6671
(609) 771-7300

NOCTI (National Occupational Competency Testing Institute) assessments are designed for people like Alice, who have vocational-technical skills that cannot be evaluated by other tests. NOCTI assesses competency at two levels: Student/job ready and teacher/experienced worker. Standardized evaluations are available for occupations such as auto-body repair, electronics, mechanical drafting, quantity food preparation, and upholstering. The tests consist of multiple-choice questions and a performance component. Other services include workshops, customized assessments, and pre-testing. For more information, contact:

NOCTI
500 N. Bronson Ave.
Ferris State University
Big Rapids, MI 49307
(616) 796-4699

Colleges and universities:

Many colleges and universities have credit-by-exam programs, through which students earn credit by passing a comprehensive exam for a course offered by the institution. Among the most widely recognized are the programs at Ohio University, the University of North Carolina, Thomas Edison State College, and New York University.

Ohio University offers about 150 examinations for credit. In addition, you may sometimes arrange to take special examinations in non-laboratory courses offered at Ohio University. To take a test for credit, you must enroll in the course. If you plan to transfer the credit earned, you also need written permission from an official at your school. Books and study materials are available, for a cost, through the university. Exams must be taken within 6 months of the enrollment date; most last 3 hours. You may arrange to take the exam off campus if you do not live near the university.

Ohio University is on the quarter-hour system; most courses are worth 4 quarter hours, the equivalent of 3 semester hours. For more information, contact:

Independent Study
Tupper Hall 302
Ohio University
Athens, OH 45701-2979
1(800) 444-2910
(614) 593-2910

The University of North Carolina offers a credit-by-examination option for 140 independent study (correspondence) courses in foreign languages, humanities, social sciences, mathematics, business administration, education, electrical and computer engineering, health administration, and natural sciences. To take an exam, you must request and receive approval from both the course instructor and the independent studies department. Exams must be taken within six months of enrollment, and you may register for no more than two at a time. If you are not near the University's Chapel Hill campus, you may take your exam under supervision at an accredited college, university, community college, or technical institute. For more information, contact:

Independent Studies
CB #1020, The Friday Center
UNC-Chapel Hill
Chapel Hill, NC 27599-1020
1(800) 862-5669 / (919) 962-1134

The Thomas Edison College Examination Program offers more than 50 exams in liberal arts, business, and professional areas. Thomas Edison State College administers tests twice a month in Trenton, New Jersey; however, students may arrange to take their tests with a proctor at any accredited American college or university or U.S. military base. Most of the tests are multiple choice; some also include short answer or essay questions. Time limits range from 90 minutes to 4 hours, depending on the exam. For more information, contact:

Thomas Edison State College
TECEP, Office of Testing and Assessment
101 W. State Street
Trenton, NJ 08608-1176
(609) 633-2844

New York University's Foreign Language Program offers proficiency exams in more than 40 languages, from Albanian to Yiddish. Two exams are available in each language: The 12-point test is equivalent to 4 undergraduate semesters, and the 16-point exam may lead to upper level credit. The tests are given at the university's Foreign Language Department throughout the year.

Proof of foreign language proficiency does not guarantee college credit. Some colleges and universities accept transcripts only for languages commonly taught, such as French and Spanish. Nontraditional programs are more likely than traditional ones to grant credit for proficiency in other languages.

For an informational brochure and registration form for NYU's foreign language proficiency exams, contact:

New York University
Foreign Language Department
48 Cooper Square, Room 107
New York, NY 10003
(212) 998-7030

Government institutes:

The Defense Language Institute and Foreign Service Institute administer foreign language proficiency exams for personnel stationed abroad. Usually, the tests are given at the end of intensive language courses or upon completion of service overseas. But some people – like Jorge, who knows Spanish – speak another language fluently and may be allowed to take a proficiency exam in that language before completing their tour of duty. Contact one of the offices listed below to obtain transcripts of those scores. Proof of proficiency does not guarantee college credit, however, as discussed above.

To request score reports from the Defense Language Institute for Defense Language Proficiency Tests, send your name, Social Security number, language for which you were tested, and, most importantly, when and where you took the exam to:

Commandant, Defense Language Institute
Attn: ATFL-ES-T
DLPT Score Report Request
Presidio of Monterey
Monterey, CA 93944-5006

To request transcripts of scores for Foreign Service Institute exams, send your name, Social Security number, language for which you were tested, and dates or year of exams to:

Foreign Service Institute
Arlington Hall
4020 Arlington Boulevard
Rosslyn, VA 22204-1500
Attn: Testing Office (Send your request to the attention of the testing office of the foreign language in which you were tested)

Credit For Experience

Experiential learning credit may be given for knowledge gained through job responsibilities, personal hobbies, volunteer opportunities, homemaking, and other experiences. Colleges and universities base credit awards on the knowledge you have attained, not for the experience alone. In addition, the knowledge must be college level; not just any learning will do. Throwing horseshoes as a hobby is not likely to be worth college credit. But if you've done research on how and where the sport originated, visited blacksmiths, organized tournaments, and written a column for a trade journal – well, that's a horseshoe of a different color.

Adults attempting to get credit for their experience should be forewarned: Having your experience evaluated for college credit is time-consuming, tedious work – not an easy shortcut for people who want quick-fix college credits. And not all experience, no matter how valuable, is the equivalent of college courses.

Requesting college credit for your experiential learning can be tricky. You should get assistance from a credit evaluations officer at the school you plan to attend, but you should also have a general idea of what your knowledge is worth. A common method for converting knowledge into credit is to use a college catalog. Find course titles and descriptions that match what you have learned through experience, and request the number of credits offered for those courses.

Once you know what credit to ask for, you must usually present your case in writing to officials at the college you plan to attend. The most common form of presenting experiential learning for credit is the portfolio. A portfolio is a written record of your knowledge along with a request for equivalent college credit. It includes an identification and description of the knowledge for which you are requesting credit, an explanatory essay of how the knowledge was gained and how it fits into your educational plans, documentation that you have acquired such knowledge, and a request for college credit. Required elements of a portfolio vary by schools but generally follow those guidelines.

In identifying knowledge you have gained, be specific about exactly what you have learned. For example, it is not enough for Lynette to say she runs a business. She must identify the knowledge she has gained from running it, such as personnel management, tax law, marketing strategy, and inventory review. She must also include brief descriptions about her knowledge of each to support her claims of having those skills.

The essay gives you a chance to relay something about who you are. It should address your educational goals, include relevant autobiographical details, and be well organized, neat, and convey confidence. In his essay, Jorge might first state his goal of becoming an engineer. Then he would explain why he joined the Army, where he got hands-on training and experience in developing and servicing electronic equipment.

This, he would say, led to his hobby of creating remote-controlled model cars, of which he has built 20. His conclusion would highlight his accomplishments and tie them to his desire to become an electronic engineer.

Documentation is evidence that you've learned what you claim to have learned. You can show proof of knowledge in a variety of ways, including audio or video recordings, letters from current or former employers describing your specific duties and job performance, blueprints, photographs or artwork, and transcripts of certifying exams for professional licenses and certification – such as Alice's certification from the American Culinary Federation. Although documentation can take many forms, written proof alone is not always enough. If it is impossible to document your knowledge in writing, find out if your experiential learning can be assessed through supplemental oral exams by a faculty expert.

Earning a College Degree

Nontraditional students often have work, family, and financial obligations that prevent them from quitting their jobs to attend school full time. Can they still meet their educational goals? Yes.

More than 150 accredited colleges and universities have nontraditional bachelor's degree programs that require students to spend little or no time on campus; over 300 others have nontraditional campus-based degree programs. Some of those schools, as well as most junior and community colleges, offer associate's degrees nontraditionally. Each school with a nontraditional course of study determines its own rules for awarding credit for prior coursework, exams, or experience, as discussed previously. Most have charges on top of tuition for providing these special services.

Several publications profile nontraditional degree programs; see the Resources section at the end of this article for more information. To determine which school best fits your academic profile and educational goals, first list your criteria. Then, evaluate nontraditional programs based on their accreditation, features, residency requirements, and expenses. Once you have chosen several schools to explore further, write to them for more information. Detailed explanations of school policies should help you decide which ones you want to apply to.

Get beyond the printed word – especially the glowing words each school writes about itself. Check out the schools you are considering with higher education authorities, alumni, employers, family members, and friends. If possible, visit the campus to talk to students and instructors and sit in on a few classes, even if you will be completing most or all of your work off campus. Ask school officials questions about such things as enrollment numbers, graduation rate, faculty qualifications, and confusing details about the application process or academic policies. After you have thoroughly investigated each prospective college or university, you can make an informed decision about which is right for you.

Accreditation

Accreditation is a process colleges and universities submit to voluntarily for getting their credentials. An accredited school has been investigated and visited by teams of observers and has periodic inspections by a private accrediting agency. The initial review can take two years or more.

Regional agencies accredit entire schools, and professional agencies accredit either specialized schools or departments within schools. Although there are no national accrediting standards, not just any accreditation will do. Countless "accreditation associations" have been invented by schools, many of which have no academic programs and sell phony degrees, to accredit themselves. But 6 regional and about 80 professional accrediting associations in the United States are recognized by the U.S. Department of Education or the Commission on Recognition of Postsecondary Accreditation. When checking accreditation, these are the names to look for. For more information about accreditation and accrediting agencies, contact:

Institutional Participation Oversight Service Accreditation and State Liaison Division
U.S. Department of Education
ROB 3, Room 3915
600 Independence Ave., SW
Washington, DC 20202-5244
(202) 708-7417

Because accreditation is not mandatory, lack of accreditation does not necessarily mean a school or program is bad. Some schools choose not to apply for accreditation, are in the process of applying, or have educational methods too unconventional for an accrediting association's standards. For the nontraditional student, however, earning a degree from a college or university with recognized accreditation is an especially important consideration. Although nontraditional education is becoming more widely accepted, it is not yet mainstream. Employers skeptical of a degree earned in a nontraditional manner are likely to be even less accepting of one from an unaccredited school.

Program Features

Because nontraditional students have diverse educational objectives, nontraditional schools are diverse in what they offer. Some programs are geared toward helping students organize their scattered educational credits to get a degree as quickly as possible. Others cater to those who may have specific credits or experience but need assistance in completing requirements. Whatever your educational profile, you should look for a program that works with you in obtaining your educational goals.

A few nontraditional programs have special admissions policies for adult learners like Alice, who plan to earn their GEDs but want to enroll in college in the meantime. Other features of nontraditional programs include individualized learning agreements, intensive academic counseling, cooperative learning and internship placement, and waiver of some prerequisites or other requirements – as well as college credit for prior coursework, examinations, and experiential learning, all discussed previously.

Lynette, whose primary goal is to finish her degree, wants to earn maximum credits for her business experience. She will look for programs that do not limit the number of credits awarded for equivalency exams and experiential learning. And since well-documented proof of knowledge is essential for earning experiential learning credits, Lynette should make sure the program she chooses provides assistance to students submitting a portfolio.

Jorge, on the other hand, has more credits than he needs in certain areas and is willing to forego some. To become an engineer, he must have a bachelor's degree; but because he is accustomed to hands-on learning, Jorge is interested in getting experience as he gains more technical skills. He will concentrate on finding schools with strong cooperative education, supervised fieldwork, or internship programs.

Residency Requirements

Programs are sometimes deemed nontraditional because of their residency requirements. Many people think of residency for colleges and universities in terms of tuition, with in-state students paying less than out-of-state ones. Residency also may refer to where a student lives, either on or off campus, while attending school.

But in nontraditional education, residency usually refers to how much time students must spend on campus, regardless of whether they attend classes there. In some nontraditional programs, students need not ever step foot on campus. Others require only a very short residency, such as one day or a few weeks. Many schools have standard residency requirements of several semesters but schedule classes for evenings or weekends to accommodate working adults.

Lynette, who previously took courses by independent study, prefers to earn credits by distance study. She will focus on schools that have no residency requirement. Several colleges and universities have nonresident degree completion programs for adults with some college credit. Under the direction of a faculty advisor, students devise a plan for earning their remaining credits. Methods for earning credits include independent study, distance learning, seminars, supervised fieldwork, and group study at arranged sites. Students may have to earn a certain number of credits through the degree-granting institution. But many programs allow students to take courses at accredited schools of their choice for transfer toward their degree.

Alice wants to attend lectures but has an unpredictable schedule. Her best course of action will be to seek out short residency programs that require students to attend seminars once or twice a semester. She can take courses that are televised and videotape them to watch when her schedule permits, with the seminars helping to ensure that she properly completes her coursework. Many colleges and universities with short residency requirements also permit students to earn some credits elsewhere, by whatever means the student chooses.

Some fields of study require classroom instruction. As Jorge will discover, few colleges and universities allow students to earn a bachelor's degree in engineering entirely through independent study. Nontraditional residency programs are designed to accommodate adults' daytime work schedules. Jorge should look for programs offering evening, weekend, summer, and accelerated courses.

Tuition and Other Expenses

The final decisions about which schools Alice, Jorge, and Lynette attend may hinge in large part on a single issue: Cost. And rising tuition is only part of the equation. Beginning with application fees and continuing through graduation fees, college expenses add up.

Traditional and nontraditional students have some expenses in common, such as the cost of books and other materials. Tuition might even be the same for some courses, especially for colleges and universities offering standard ones at unusual times. But for nontraditional programs, students may also pay fees for services such as credit or transcript review, evaluation, advisement, and portfolio assessment.

Students are also responsible for postage and handling or setup expenses for independent study courses, as well as for all examination and transcript fees for transferring credits. Usually, the more nontraditional the program, the more detailed the fees. Some schools charge a yearly enrollment fee rather than tuition for degree completion candidates who want their files to remain active.

Although tuition and fees might seem expensive, most educators tell you not to let money come between you and your educational goals. Talk to someone in the financial aid department of the school you plan to attend or check your library for publications about financial aid sources. The U.S. Department of Education publishes a guide to Federal aid programs such as Pell Grants, student loans, and work-study. To order the free 74-page booklet, *The Student Guide: Financial Aid from the U.S. Department of Education*, contact:

Federal Student Aid Information Center
P.O. Box 84
Washington, DC 20044
1 (800) 4FED-AID (433-3243)

Resources

Information on how to earn a high school diploma or college degree without following the usual routes is available from several organizations and in numerous publications. Information on nontraditional graduate degree programs, available for master's through doctoral level, though not discussed in this article, can usually be obtained from the same resources that detail bachelor's degree programs.

National Learning Corporation publishes study guides for all of these exams, for both general examinations and tests in specific subject areas. To order study guides, or to browse their catalog featuring more than 5,000 titles, visit NLC online at www.passbooks.com, or contact them by phone at (800) 632-8888.

Organizations

Adult learners should always contact their local school system, community college, or university to learn about programs that are readily available. The following national organizations can also supply information:

American Council on Education
One Dupont Circle
Washington, DC 20036-1193
(202) 939-9300

Within the American Council on Education, the Center for Adult Learning and Educational Credentials administers the National External Diploma Program, the GED Program, the Program on Noncollegiate Sponsored Instruction, the Credit by Examination Program, and the Military Evaluations Program.

DANTES Subject Standardized Tests

INTRODUCTION

The DANTES (Defense Activity for Non-Traditional Education Support) subject standardized tests are comprehensive college and graduate level examinations given by the Armed Forces, colleges and graduate schools as end-of-subject course evaluation final examinations or to obtain college equivalency credits in the various subject areas tested.

The DANTES Examination Program enables students to obtain college credit for what they have learned on the job, through self-study, personal interest, correspondence courses or by any other means. It is used by colleges and universities to award college credit to students who demonstrate that they know as much as students completing an equivalent college course. It is a cost-efficient, time-saving way for students to use their knowledge to accomplish their educational goals.

Most schools accept the American Council on Education (ACE) recommendations for the minimum score required and the amount of credit awarded, but not all schools do. Be sure to check the policy regarding the score level required for credit and the number of credits to be awarded.

Not all tests are accepted by all institutions. Even when a test is accepted by an institution, it may not be acceptable for every program at that institution. Before considering testing, ascertain the acceptability of a specific test for a particular course.

Colleges and universities that administer DANTES tests may administer them to any applicant – or they may administer the tests only to students registered at their institution. Decisions about who will be allowed to test are made by the school. Students should contact the test center to determine current policies and schedules for DANTES testing.

Colleges and universities authorized to administer DANTES tests usually do so throughout the calendar year. Each school sets its own fee for test administration and establishes its own testing schedule. Contact the representative at the administering school directly to make arrangements for testing.

Checklist

For Students

✓ Visit **www.getcollegecredit.com** to obtain a list of tests, fact sheets, test preparation materials, participating colleges and universities, and much more.

✓ Contact your school advisor to confirm that the DSST you selected will fit into your curriculum.

✓ Consult the *DSST Candidate Information Bulletin* for answers to specific questions.

✓ Contact the test site to schedule your test.

✓ Prepare for your examination by using the fact sheet as a guide.

✓ Take the test.

If you would like a score report sent to your college or university, it is a good idea to bring the four-digit code with you. You must write the DSST Test Center Code for that institution on your answer sheet at the time of testing. DSST Test Center Codes are noted in the DSST Participating Colleges and Universities listing on the Web site.

If you prefer to send a score report to an institution at a later date, there is a transcript fee of $20 for each transcript ordered.

Thomson Prometric
DSST Program
2000 Lenox Drive, Third Floor
Lawrenceville, NJ 08648

Toll-free: 877-471-9860
609-895-5011

E-mail: pnj-dsst@thomson.com

MAKING A COLLEGE DEGREE WITHIN YOUR REACH

Today, there are many educational alternatives to the classroom—you can learn from your job, your reading, your independent study, and special interests you pursue. You may already have learned the subject matter covered by some college-level courses.

The DSST Program is a nationally recognized testing program that gives you the opportunity to receive college credit for learning acquired outside the traditional college classroom. Colleges and universities throughout the United States administer the program, developed by Thomson Prometric, year-round. Annually, over 90,000 DSSTs are administered to individuals who are interested in continuing their education. Take advantage of the DSST testing program; it speeds the educational process and provides the flexibility adults need, making earning a degree more feasible.

Since requirements differ from college to college, please check with the credit-awarding institution before taking a DSST. More than 1,800 colleges and universities currently award credit for DSSTs, and the number is growing every day. You can choose from 37 test titles in the areas of Social Science, Business, Mathematics, Applied Technology, Humanities, and Physical Science. A brief description of each examination is found on the pages that follow.

Reach Your Career Goals Through DSSTs

Use DSSTs to help you earn your degree, get a promotion, or simply demonstrate that you have college-level knowledge in subjects relevant to your work.

Save Time...

You don't have to sit through classes when you have previously acquired the knowledge or experience for most of what is being taught and can learn the rest yourself. You might be able to bypass introductory-level courses in subject areas you already know.

Save Money...

DSSTs save you money because the classes you bypass by earning credit through the DSST Program are classes you won't have to pay for on your way to earning your degree. You can use the money instead to take more advanced courses that can be more challenging and rewarding.

Improve Your Chances for Admission to College

Each college has its own admission policies; however, having passing scores for DSSTs on your transcript can provide strong evidence of how well you can perform at the college level.

Gain Confidence Performing at a College Level

Many adults returning to college find that lack of confidence is often the greatest hurdle to overcome. Passing a DSST demonstrates your ability to perform on a college level.

Make Up for Courses You May Have Missed

You may be ready to graduate from college and find that you are a few credits short of earning your degree. By using semester breaks, vacation time, or leisure time to study independently, you can prepare to take one or more DSSTs, fulfill your academic requirements, and graduate on time.

If You Cannot Attend Regularly Scheduled Classes...

If your lifestyle or responsibilities prevent you from attending regularly scheduled classes, you can earn your college degree from a college offering an external degree program. The DSST Program allows you to earn your degree by study and experience outside the traditional classroom.

Many colleges and universities offer external degree or distance learning programs. For additional information, contact the college you plan to attend or:

Center for Lifelong Learning
American Council on Education
One DuPont Circle NW, Suite 250
Washington, DC 20036
202-939-9475
www.acenet.edu
(Select "Center for Lifelong Learning" under "Programs & Services"
for more information)

Fact Sheets

For each test, there is a Fact Sheet that outlines the topics covered by each test and includes a list of sample questions, a list of recommended references of books that would be useful for review, and the number of credits awarded for a passing score as recommended by the American Council on Education (ACE). *Please note that some schools require scores that are higher than the minimum ACE-recommended passing score.* It is suggested that you check with your college or university to determine what score they require in order to earn credit. You can obtain Fact Sheets by:
- Downloading them from www.getcollegecredit.com
- E-mailing a request to pnj-dsst@thomson.com
- Completing a Candidate Publications Order Form

DSST Online Practice Tests

DSST online practice tests contain items that reflect a *partial range of difficulty* identified in the Content Outline section on each Fact Sheet. There is an online DSST Practice Test in the following categories:
- Mathematics
- Social Science
- Business
- Physical Science
- Applied Technology
- Humanities

Although the online DSST Practice Test questions do not indicate the full range of difficulty you would find in an actual DSST test, they will help you assess your knowledge level. Each online DSST Practice Test can be purchased by visiting www.getcollegecredit.com and clicking on DSST Practice Exams.

TAKING DSST EXAMINATIONS

Earning College Credit for DSST Examinations

To find out if the college of your choice awards credit for passing DSST scores, contact the admissions office or counseling and testing office. The college can also provide information on the scores required for awarding credit, the number of credit hours awarded, and any courses that can be bypassed with satisfactory scores.

It is important that you contact the institution of your choice as early as possible since credit-awarding policies differ among colleges and universities.

Where to Take DSSTs

DSSTs are administered at colleges and universities nationwide. Each location determines the frequency and scheduling of test administrations. To obtain the most current list of participating DSST colleges and universities:

- Visit and download the information from www.getcollegecredit.com
- E-mail pnj-dsst@thomson.com

Scheduling Your Examination

Please be aware that some colleges and universities provide DSST testing services to enrolled students only. After you have selected a college or university that administers DSSTs, you will need to contact them to schedule your test date.

The fee to take a DSST is $60 per test. This fee entitles you to two score reports after the test is scored. One will be sent directly to you and the other will be sent to the college or university that you designate on your answer sheet. You may pay the test fee with a certified check or U.S. money order made payable to Thomson Prometric or you may charge the test fee to your Visa, MasterCard or American Express credit card. Note: The credit card statement will reflect a charge from Thomson Prometric for all DSST examinations. *(Declined credit card charges will be assessed an additional $25 processing fee.)*

In addition, the test site may also require a test administration fee for each examination, to be paid directly to the institution. Contact the test site to determine its administration fee and payment policy.

Other Testing Arrangements

If you are unable to find a participating DSST college or university in your area, you may want to contact the testing office of a local accredited college or university to determine whether a representative from that office will agree to administer the test(s) for you.

The school's representative should then contact the DSST Program at 866-794-3497 to arrange for this administration. If you are unable to locate a test site, contact Thomson Prometric for assistance at pnj-dsst@thomson.com or 866-794-3497.

Testing Accommodations for Students with Disabilities

Thomson Prometric is committed to serving test takers with disabilities by providing services and reasonable testing accommodations as set forth in the provisions of the *Americans with Disabilities Act* (ADA). If you have a disability, as prescribed by the ADA, and require special testing services or arrangements, please contact the test administrator at the test site. You will be asked to submit to the test administrator documentation of your disability and your request for special accommodations. The test administrator will then forward your documentation along with your request for testing accommodations to Thomson Prometric for approval.

Please submit your request as far in advance of your test date as possible so that the necessary accommodations can be made. Only test takers with documented disabilities are eligible for special accommodations.

On the Day of the Examination

It is important to review this information and to have the correct identification present on the day of the examination:

- Arrive on time as a courtesy to the test administrator.
- Bring a valid form of government-issued identification that includes a current photo and your signature (acceptable documents include a driver's license, passport, state-issued identification card or military identification). *Anyone who fails to present valid identification will not be allowed to test.*
- Bring several No. 2 (soft-lead) sharpened pencils with good erasers, a watch, and a black pen if you will be writing an essay.
- Do not bring books or papers.
- Do not bring an alarm watch that beeps, a telephone, or a phone beeper into the testing room.
- The use of nonprogrammable calculators, slide rules, scratch paper and/or other materials is permitted for some of the tests.

DSST SCORING POLICIES

Your DSST examination scores are reported only to you, unless you request that they be sent elsewhere. If you want your scores sent to your college, you must provide the correct DSST code number of the school on your answer sheet at the time you take the test. See the *DSST Directory of Colleges and Universities* on the Web site www.getcollegecredit.com.

If your institution is not listed, contact Thomson Prometric at 866-794-3497 to establish a code number. (Some schools may require a student to be enrolled prior to receiving a score report.)

Receiving Your Score Report

Allow approximately four weeks after testing to receive your score report.

Calling DSST Customer Service before the required four-week score processing time has elapsed will not expedite the processing of your scores. Due to privacy and security requirements, scores will not be reported to students over the telephone under any circumstance.

Scoring of Principles of Public Speaking Speeches

The speech portion of the *Principles of Public Speaking* examination will be sent to speech raters who are faculty members at accredited colleges that currently teach or have previously taught the course. Scores for the *Principles of Public Speaking* examination are available six to eight weeks from receipt by Thomson Prometric. If you take the *Principles of Public Speaking* examination and fail (either the objective, speech portion, or both), you must follow the retesting policy waiting period of six months (180 days) before retaking the entire exam.

Essays

The essays for *Ethics in America* and *Technical Writing* are <u>optional</u> and thus are not scored by raters. The essays are forwarded to the college or university that you designate, along with your score report, for their use in determining the award of credit. <u>Before taking the *Ethics in America* or *Technical Writing* examinations, check with your college or university to determine whether the essay is required.</u>

NOTE: *Principles of Public Speaking* speech topic cassette tapes and essays are kept on file at Thomson Prometric for one year from the date of administration.

How to Get Transcripts

There is a $20 fee for each transcript you request. Payment must be in the form of a certified check, U.S. money order payable to Thomson Prometric, or credit card. Personal checks and debit cards are NOT an acceptable method of payment. One transcript may include scores for one or more examinations taken. To request a transcript, download the Transcript Order Form from www.getcollegecredit.com.

DESCRIPTION OF THE DSST EXAMINATIONS

Mathematics

• **Fundamentals of College Algebra** covers mathematical concepts such as fundamental algebraic operations; linear, absolute value; quadratic equations, inequalities, radials, exponents and logarithms, factoring polynomials and graphing. The use of a nonprogrammable, handheld calculator is permitted.

• **Principles of Statistics** tests the understanding of the various topics of statistics, both qualitatively and quantitatively, and the ability to apply statistical methods to solve a variety of problems. The topics included in this test are descriptive statistics; correlation and regression; probability; chance models and sampling and tests of significance. The use of a nonprogrammable, handheld calculator is permitted.

Social Science

• **Art of the Western World** deals with the history of art during the following periods: classical; Romanesque and Gothic; early Renaissance; high Renaissance, Baroque; rococo; neoclassicism and romanticism; realism, impressionism and post-impressionism; early twentieth century; and post-World War II.

• **Western Europe Since 1945** tests the knowledge of basic facts and terms and the understanding of concepts and principles related to the areas of the historical background of the aftermath of the Second World War and rebuilding of Europe; national political systems; issues and policies in Western European societies; European institutions and processes; and Europe's relations with the rest of the world.

• **An Introduction to the Modern Middle East** emphasizes core knowledge (including geography, Judaism, Christianity, Islam, ethnicity); nineteenth-century European impact; twentieth-century Western influences; World Wars I and II; new nations; social and cultural changes (1900-1960) and the Middle East from 1960 to present.

• **Human/Cultural Geography** includes the Earth and basic facts (coordinate systems, maps, physiography, atmosphere, soils and vegetation, water); culture and environment, spatial processes (social processes, modern economic systems, settlement patterns, political geography); and regional geography.

- **Rise and Fall of the Soviet Union** covers Russia under the Old Regime; the Revolutionary Period; New Economic Policy; Pre-war Stalinism; The Second World War; Post-war Stalinism; The Khrushchev Years; The Brezhnev Era; and reform and collapse.

- **A History of the Vietnam War** covers the history of the roots of the Vietnam War; the First Vietnam War (1946-1954); pre-war developments (1954-1963); American involvement in the Vietnam War; Tet (1968); Vietnamizing the War (1968-1973); Cambodia and Laos; peace; legacies and lessons.

- **The Civil War and Reconstruction** covers the Civil War from presecession (1861) through Reconstruction. It includes causes of the war; secession; Fort Sumter; the war in the east and in the west; major battles; the political situation; assassination of Lincoln; end of the Confederacy; and Reconstruction.

- **Foundations of Education** includes topics such as contemporary issues in education; past and current influences on education (philosophies, democratic ideals, social/economic influences); and the interrelationships between contemporary issues and influences.

- **Life-span Developmental Psychology** covers models and theories; methods of study; ethical issues; biological development; perception, learning and memory; cognition and language; social, emotional, and personality development; social behaviors, family life cycle, extrafamilial settings; singlehood and cohabitation; occupational development and retirement; adjustment to life stresses; and bereavement and loss.

- **Drug and Alcohol Abuse** includes such topics as drug use in society; classification of drugs; pharmacological principles; alcohol (types, effects of, alcoholism); general principles and use of sedative hypnotics, narcotic analgesics, stimulants, and hallucinogens; other drugs (inhalants, steroids); and prevention/treatment.

- **General Anthropology** deals with anthropology as a discipline; theoretical perspectives; physical anthropology; archaeology; social organization; economic organization; political organization; religion; and modernization and application of anthropology.

- **Introduction to Law Enforcement** includes topics such as history and professional movement of law enforcement; overview of the U.S. criminal justice system; police systems in the U.S.; police organization, management, and issues; and U.S. law and precedents.

- **Criminal Justice** deals with criminal behavior (crime in the U.S., theories of crime, types of crime); the criminal justice system (historical origins, legal foundations, due process); police; the court system (history and organization, adult court system, juvenile court, pre-trial and post-trial processes); and corrections.

- **Fundamentals of Counseling** covers historical development (significant influences and people); counselor roles and functions; the counseling relationship; and theoretical approaches to counseling.

Business
- **Principles of Finance** deals with financial statements and planning; time value of money; working capital management; valuation and characteristics; capital budgeting; cost of capital; risk and return; and international financial management. The use of a nonprogrammable, handheld calculator is permitted.

• **Principles of Financial Accounting** includes topics such as general concepts and principles, accounting cycle and classification; transaction analysis; accruals and deferrals; cash and internal control; current accounts; long- and short-term liabilities; capital stock; and financial statements. The use of a nonprogrammable, handheld calculator is permitted.

• **Human Resource Management** covers general employment issues; job analysis; training and development; performance appraisals; compensation issues; security issues; personnel legislation and regulation; labor relations and current issues; an overview of the Human Resource Management Field; Human Resource Planning; Staffing; training and development; compensation issues; safety and health; employee rights and discipline; employment law; labor relations and current issues and trends.

• **Organizational Behavior** deals with the study of organizational behavior (scientific approaches, research designs, data collection methods); individual processes and characteristics; interpersonal and group processes and characteristics; organizational processes and characteristics; and change and development processes.

• **Principles of Supervision** deals with the roles and responsibilities of the supervisor; management functions (planning, organization and staffing, directing at the supervisory level); and other topics (legal issues, stress management, union environments, quality concerns).

• **Business Law II** covers topics such as sales of goods; debtor and creditor relations; business organizations; property; and commercial paper.

• **Introduction to Computing** includes topics such as history and technological generations; hardware/software; applications to information technology; program development; data management; communications and connectivity; and computing and society. The use of a nonprogrammable, handheld calculator is permitted.

• **Management Information Systems** covers systems theory, analysis and design of systems, hardware and software; database management; telecommunications; management of the MIS functional area and informational support.

• **Introduction to Business** deals with economic issues affecting business; international business; government and business; forms of business ownership; small business, entrepreneurship and franchise; management process; human resource management; production and operations; marketing management; financial management; risk management and insurance; and management and information systems.

• **Money and Banking** covers the role and kinds of money; commercial banks and other financial intermediaries; central banking and the Federal Reserve system; money and macroeconomics activity; monetary policy in the U.S.; and the international monetary system.

• **Personal Finance** includes topics such as financial goals and values; budgeting; credit and debt; major purchases; taxes; insurance; investments; and retirement and estate planning. The use of auxiliary materials, such as calculators and slide rules, is NOT permitted.

• **Business Mathematics** deals with basic operations with integers, fractions, and decimals; round numbers; ratios; averages; business graphs; simple interest; compound interest and annuities; net pay and deductions; discounts and markups; depreciation and net worth; corporate securities; distribution of ownership; and stock and asset turnover.

Physical Science
• **Astronomy** covers the history of astronomy, celestial mechanics; celestial systems; astronomical instruments; the solar system; nature and evolution; the galaxy; the universe; determining astronomical distances; and life in the universe.

• **Here's to Your Health** covers mental health and behavior; human development and relationships; substance abuse; fitness and nutrition; risk factors, disease, and disease prevention; and safety, consumer awareness, and environmental concerns.

• **Environment and Humanity** deals with topics such as ecological concepts (ecosystems, global ecology, food chains and webs); environmental impacts; environmental management and conservation; and political processes and the future.

• **Principles of Physical Science I** includes physics: Newton's Laws of Motion; energy and momentum; thermodynamics; wave and optics; electricity and magnetism; chemistry: properties of matter; atomic theory and structure; and chemical reactions.

• **Physical Geology** covers Earth materials; igneous, sedimentary, and metamorphic rocks; surface processes (weathering, groundwater, glaciers, oceanic systems, deserts and winds, hydrologic cycle); internal Earth processes; and applications (mineral and energy resources, environmental geology).

Applied Technology
• **Technical Writing** covers topics such as theory and practice of technical writing; purpose, content, and organizational patterns of common types of technical documents; elements of various technical reports; and technical editing. Students have the option to write a short essay on one of the technical topics provided. Thomson Prometric will not score the essay; however, for determining the award of credit, a copy of the essay will be forwarded to the college or university you've designated along with the score report or transcript.

Humanities
• **Ethics in America** deals with ethical traditions (Greek views, Biblical traditions, moral law, consequential ethics, feminist ethics); ethical analysis of issues arising in interpersonal and personal-societal relationships and in professional and occupational roles; and relationships between ethical traditions and the ethical analysis of situations. Students have the option to write an essay to analyze a morally problematic situation in terms of issues relevant to a decision and arguments for alternative positions. Thomson Prometric will not score the essay; however, for determining the award of credit, a copy of the essay will be forwarded to the college or university you've designated along with the score report or transcript.

• **Introduction to World Religions** covers topics such as dimensions and approaches to religion; primal religions; Hinduism; Buddhism; Confucianism; Taoism; Judaism; Christianity; and Islam.

• **Principles of Public Speaking** consists of two parts: Part One consists of multiple-choice questions covering considerations of Principles of Public Speaking; audience analysis; purposes of speeches; structure/organization; content/supporting materials; research; language and style; delivery; communication apprehension; listening and feedback; and criticism and evaluation. Part Two requires the student to record an impromptu persuasive speech that will be scored.

FREQUENTLY ASKED QUESTIONS ABOUT DSSTs

In order to pass the test, must I study from one of the recommended references?

The recommended references are a listing of books that were being used as textbooks in college courses of the same or similar title at the time the test was developed. Appropriate textbooks for study are not limited to those listed in the fact sheet. If you wish to obtain study resources to prepare for the examination, you may reference either the current edition of the listed titles or textbooks currently used at a local college or university for the same class title. It is recommended that you reference more than one textbook on the topics outlined in the fact sheet. You should begin by checking textbook content against the content outline included on the front page of the DSST fact sheet before selecting textbooks that cover the text content from which to study. Textbooks may be found at the campus bookstore of a local college or university offering a course on the subject.

Is there a penalty for guessing on the tests?

There is no penalty for guessing on DSSTs, so you should mark an answer for each question.

How much time will I have to complete the test?

Many DSSTs can be completed within 90 minutes; however, additional time can be allowed if necessary.

What should I do if I find a test question irregularity?

Continue testing and then report the irregularity to the test administrator after the test. This may be done by asking that the test administrator note the irregularity on the Supervisor's Irregularity Report or you can write to Thomson Prometric, DSST Program, 2000 Lenox Drive, Third Floor, Lawrenceville, NJ 08648, and indicate the form and question number(s) or circumstances as well as your name and address.

When will I receive my score report?

Allow approximately four weeks from the date of testing to receive your score report. Allow six to eight weeks to receive a score report for the *Principles of Public Speaking* examination.

Will my test scores be released without my permission?

Your test score will not be released to anyone other than the school you designate on your answer sheet unless you write to us and ask us to send a transcript elsewhere. Instructions about how to do this can be found on your score report. Your scores may be used for research purposes, but individual scores are never made public nor are individuals identified if research findings are made public.

If I do not achieve a passing score on the test, how long must I wait until I can take the test again?

If you do not receive a score on the test that will enable you to obtain credit for the course, you may take the test again after six months (180 days). Please do not attempt to take the test before six months (180 days) have passed because you will receive a score report marked *invalid* and your test fee will not be refunded.

Can my test scores be canceled?

The test administrator is required to report any irregularities to Thomson Prometric. The consequence of bringing unauthorized materials into the testing room, or giving or receiving help, will be the forfeiture of your test fee and the invalidation of test scores. The DSST Program reserves the right to cancel scores and not issue score reports in such situations.

What can I do if I feel that my test scores were not accurately reported?

Thomson Prometric recognizes the extreme importance of test results to candidates and has a multi-step quality-control procedure to help ensure that reported scores are accurate. If you have reason to believe that your score(s) were not accurately reported, you may request to have your answer sheet reviewed and hand scored.

The fees for this service are:
• $20 fee if requested within six months of the test date
• $30 fee if requested more than six months from the test date
• $30 fee if a re-evaluation of the *Principles of Public Speaking* speech is requested

The fee for this service can be paid by credit card or by certified check or U.S. money order payable to Thomson Prometric. Submit your request for score verification along with the appropriate fee or credit card information (credit card number and expiration date) to Thomson Prometric, DSST Program, 2000 Lenox Drive, Third Floor, Lawrenceville, NJ 08648. Include your full name, the test title, the date you took the test, and your Social Security number. Candidates will be notified if a scoring discrepancy is discovered within four weeks of receipt of the request.

What does ACE recommendation mean?

The ACE recommendation is the minimum passing score recommended by the American Council on Education for any given test. It is equivalent to the average score of students in the DSST norming sample who received a grade of C for the course. Some schools require a score higher than the ACE recommendation.

Who is NLC?

National Learning Corporation (NLC) has been successfully preparing candidates for 40 years for over 5,000 exams. NLC publishes Passbook® study guides to help candidates prepare for all DANTES and CLEP exams and almost every other type of exam from high school through adult career.

Go to our website — www.passbooks.com — or call (800) 632-8888 for information about ordering our Passbooks.

To get detailed information on the DSST program and DSST preparation materials, visit www.getcollegecredit.com.

If you are interested in taking the DSST exams, call 877-471-9860 or e-mail pnj-dsst@thomson.com.

HOW TO TAKE A TEST

You have studied long, hard and conscientiously.

With your official admission card in hand, and your heart pounding, you have been admitted to the examination room.

You note that there are several hundred other applicants in the examination room waiting to take the same test.

They all appear to be equally well prepared.

You know that nothing but your best effort will suffice. The "moment of truth" is at hand: you now have to demonstrate objectively, in writing, your knowledge of content and your understanding of subject matter.

You are fighting the most important battle of your life—to pass and/or score high on an examination which will determine your career and provide the economic basis for your livelihood.

What extra, special things should you know and should you do in taking the examination?

I. YOU MUST PASS AN EXAMINATION

A. WHAT EVERY CANDIDATE SHOULD KNOW

Examination applicants often ask us for help in preparing for the written test. What can I study in advance? What kinds of questions will be asked? How will the test be given? How will the papers be graded?

B. HOW ARE EXAMS DEVELOPED?

Examinations are carefully written by trained technicians who are specialists in the field known as "psychological measurement," in consultation with recognized authorities in the field of work that the test will cover. These experts recommend the subject matter areas or skills to be tested; only those knowledges or skills important to your success on the job are included. The most reliable books and source materials available are used as references. Together, the experts and technicians judge the difficulty level of the questions.

Test technicians know how to phrase questions so that the problem is clearly stated. Their ethics do not permit "trick" or "catch" questions. Questions may have been tried out on sample groups, or subjected to statistical analysis, to determine their usefulness.

Written tests are often used in combination with performance tests, ratings of training and experience, and oral interviews. All of these measures combine to form the best-known means of finding the right person for the right job.

II. HOW TO PASS THE WRITTEN TEST

A. BASIC STEPS

1) Study the announcement

How, then, can you know what subjects to study? Our best answer is: "Learn as much as possible about the class of positions for which you've applied." The exam will test the knowledge, skills and abilities needed to do the work.

Your most valuable source of information about the position you want is the official exam announcement. This announcement lists the training and experience qualifications. Check these standards and apply only if you come reasonably close to meeting them. Many jurisdictions preview the written test in the exam announcement by including a section called "Knowledge and Abilities Required," "Scope of the Examination," or some similar heading. Here you will find out specifically what fields will be tested.

2) Choose appropriate study materials

If the position for which you are applying is technical or advanced, you will read more advanced, specialized material. If you are already familiar with the basic principles of your field, elementary textbooks would waste your time. Concentrate on advanced textbooks and technical periodicals. Think through the concepts and review difficult problems in your field.

These are all general sources. You can get more ideas on your own initiative, following these leads. For example, training manuals and publications of the government agency which employs workers in your field can be useful, particularly for technical and professional positions. A letter or visit to the government department involved may result in more specific study suggestions, and certainly will provide you with a more definite idea of the exact nature of the position you are seeking.

3) Study this book!

III. KINDS OF TESTS

Tests are used for purposes other than measuring knowledge and ability to perform specified duties. For some positions, it is equally important to test ability to make adjustments to new situations or to profit from training. In others, basic mental abilities not dependent on information are essential. Questions which test these things may not appear as pertinent to the duties of the position as those which test for knowledge and information. Yet they are often highly important parts of a fair examination. For very general questions, it is almost impossible to help you direct your study efforts. What we can do is to point out some of the more common of these general abilities needed in public service positions and describe some typical questions.

1) General information

Broad, general information has been found useful for predicting job success in some kinds of work. This is tested in a variety of ways, from vocabulary lists to questions about current events. Basic background in some field of work, such as sociology or economics, may be sampled in a group of questions. Often these are principles which have become familiar to most persons through exposure rather than through formal training. It is difficult to advise you how to study for these questions; being alert to the world around you is our best suggestion.

2) Verbal ability

An example of an ability needed in many positions is verbal or language ability. Verbal ability is, in brief, the ability to use and understand words. Vocabulary and grammar tests are typical measures of this ability. Reading comprehension or paragraph interpretation questions are common in many kinds of civil service tests. You are given a paragraph of written material and asked to find its central meaning.

IV. KINDS OF QUESTIONS

1. Multiple-choice Questions

Most popular of the short-answer questions is the "multiple choice" or "best answer" question. It can be used, for example, to test for factual knowledge, ability to solve problems or judgment in meeting situations found at work.

A multiple-choice question is normally one of three types:
- It can begin with an incomplete statement followed by several possible endings. You are to find the one ending which *best* completes the statement, although some of the others may not be entirely wrong.
- It can also be a complete statement in the form of a question which is answered by choosing one of the statements listed.
- It can be in the form of a problem – again you select the best answer.

Here is an example of a multiple-choice question with a discussion which should give you some clues as to the method for choosing the right answer:

When an employee has a complaint about his assignment, the action which will *best* help him overcome his difficulty is to
- A. discuss his difficulty with his coworkers
- B. take the problem to the head of the organization
- C. take the problem to the person who gave him the assignment
- D. say nothing to anyone about his complaint

In answering this question, you should study each of the choices to find which is best. Consider choice "A" – Certainly an employee may discuss his complaint with fellow employees, but no change or improvement can result, and the complaint remains unresolved. Choice "B" is a poor choice since the head of the organization probably does not know what assignment you have been given, and taking your problem to him is known as "going over the head" of the supervisor. The supervisor, or person who made the assignment, is the person who can clarify it or correct any injustice. Choice "C" is, therefore, correct. To say nothing, as in choice "D," is unwise. Supervisors have and interest in knowing the problems employees are facing, and the employee is seeking a solution to his problem.

2. True/False

3. Matching Questions

Matching an answer from a column of choices within another column.

V. RECORDING YOUR ANSWERS

Computer terminals are used more and more today for many different kinds of exams.

For an examination with very few applicants, you may be told to record your answers in the test booklet itself. Separate answer sheets are much more common. If this separate answer sheet is to be scored by machine – and this is often the case – it is highly important that you mark your answers correctly in order to get credit.

VI. BEFORE THE TEST

YOUR PHYSICAL CONDITION IS IMPORTANT

If you are not well, you can't do your best work on tests. If you are half asleep, you can't do your best either. Here are some tips:

1) Get about the same amount of sleep you usually get. Don't stay up all night before the test, either partying or worrying—DON'T DO IT!
2) If you wear glasses, be sure to wear them when you go to take the test. This goes for hearing aids, too.
3) If you have any physical problems that may keep you from doing your best, be sure to tell the person giving the test. If you are sick or in poor health, you relay cannot do your best on any test. You can always come back and take the test some other time.

Common sense will help you find procedures to follow to get ready for an examination. Too many of us, however, overlook these sensible measures. Indeed, nervousness and fatigue have been found to be the most serious reasons why applicants fail to do their best on civil service tests. Here is a list of reminders:

- Begin your preparation early – Don't wait until the last minute to go scurrying around for books and materials or to find out what the position is all about.
- Prepare continuously – An hour a night for a week is better than an all-night cram session. This has been definitely established. What is more, a night a week for a month will return better dividends than crowding your study into a shorter period of time.
- Locate the place of the exam – You have been sent a notice telling you when and where to report for the examination. If the location is in a different town or otherwise unfamiliar to you, it would be well to inquire the best route and learn something about the building.
- Relax the night before the test – Allow your mind to rest. Do not study at all that night. Plan some mild recreation or diversion; then go to bed early and get a good night's sleep.
- Get up early enough to make a leisurely trip to the place for the test – This way unforeseen events, traffic snarls, unfamiliar buildings, etc. will not upset you.

- Dress comfortably – A written test is not a fashion show. You will be known by number and not by name, so wear something comfortable.
- Leave excess paraphernalia at home – Shopping bags and odd bundles will get in your way. You need bring only the items mentioned in the official notice you received; usually everything you need is provided. Do not bring reference books to the exam. They will only confuse those last minutes and be taken away from you when in the test room.
- Arrive somewhat ahead of time – If because of transportation schedules you must get there very early, bring a newspaper or magazine to take your mind off yourself while waiting.
- Locate the examination room – When you have found the proper room, you will be directed to the seat or part of the room where you will sit. Sometimes you are given a sheet of instructions to read while you are waiting. Do not fill out any forms until you are told to do so; just read them and be prepared.
- Relax and prepare to listen to the instructions
- If you have any physical problem that may keep you from doing your best, be sure to tell the test administrator. If you are sick or in poor health, you really cannot do your best on the exam. You can come back and take the test some other time.

VII. AT THE TEST

The day of the test is here and you have the test booklet in your hand. The temptation to get going is very strong. Caution! There is more to success than knowing the right answers. You must know how to identify your papers and understand variations in the type of short-answer question used in this particular examination. Follow these suggestions for maximum results from your efforts:

1) Cooperate with the monitor
The test administrator has a duty to create a situation in which you can be as much at ease as possible. He will give instructions, tell you when to begin, check to see that you are marking your answer sheet correctly, and so on. He is not there to guard you, although he will see that your competitors do not take unfair advantage. He wants to help you do your best.

2) Listen to all instructions
Don't jump the gun! Wait until you understand all directions. In most civil service tests you get more time than you need to answer the questions. So don't be in a hurry. Read each word of instructions until you clearly understand the meaning. Study the examples, listen to all announcements and follow directions. Ask questions if you do not understand what to do.

3) Identify your papers
Civil service exams are usually identified by number only. You will be assigned a number; you must not put your name on your test papers. Be sure to copy your number correctly. Since more than one exam may be given, copy your exact examination title.

4) Plan your time
Unless you are told that a test is a "speed" or "rate of work" test, speed itself is usually not important. Time enough to answer all the questions will be provided, but this

does not mean that you have all day. An overall time limit has been set. Divide the total time (in minutes) by the number of questions to determine the approximate time you have for each question.

5) Do not linger over difficult questions

If you come across a difficult question, mark it with a paper clip (useful to have along) and come back to it when you have been through the booklet. One caution if you do this – be sure to skip a number on your answer sheet as well. Check often to be sure that you have not lost your place and that you are marking in the row numbered the same as the question you are answering.

6) Read the questions

Be sure you know what the question asks! Many capable people are unsuccessful because they failed to *read* the questions correctly.

7) Answer all questions

Unless you have been instructed that a penalty will be deducted for incorrect answers, it is better to guess than to omit a question.

8) Speed tests

It is often better NOT to guess on speed tests. It has been found that on timed tests people are tempted to spend the last few seconds before time is called in marking answers at random – without even reading them – in the hope of picking up a few extra points. To discourage this practice, the instructions may warn you that your score will be "corrected" for guessing. That is, a penalty will be applied. The incorrect answers will be deducted from the correct ones, or some other penalty formula will be used.

9) Review your answers

If you finish before time is called, go back to the questions you guessed or omitted to give them further thought. Review other answers if you have time.

10) Return your test materials

If you are ready to leave before others have finished or time is called, take ALL your materials to the monitor and leave quietly. Never take any test material with you. The monitor can discover whose papers are not complete, and taking a test booklet may be grounds for disqualification.

VIII. EXAMINATION TECHNIQUES

1) Read the general instructions carefully. These are usually printed on the first page of the exam booklet. As a rule, these instructions refer to the timing of the examination; the fact that you should not start work until the signal and must stop work at a signal, etc. If there are any *special* instructions, such as a choice of questions to be answered, make sure that you note this instruction carefully.

2) When you are ready to start work on the examination, that is as soon as the signal has been given, read the instructions to each question booklet, underline any key words or phrases, such as *least, best, outline, describe*

and the like. In this way you will tend to answer as requested rather than discover on reviewing your paper that you *listed without describing*, that you selected the *worst* choice rather than the *best* choice, etc.

3) If the examination is of the objective or multiple-choice type – that is, each question will also give a series of possible answers: A, B, C or D, and you are called upon to select the best answer and write the letter next to that answer on your answer paper – it is advisable to start answering each question in turn. There may be anywhere from 50 to 100 such questions in the three or four hours allotted and you can see how much time would be taken if you read through all the questions before beginning to answer any. Furthermore, if you come across a question or group of questions which you know would be difficult to answer, it would undoubtedly affect your handling of all the other questions.

4) If the examination is of the essay type and contains but a few questions, it is a moot point as to whether you should read all the questions before starting to answer any one. Of course, if you are given a choice – say five out of seven and the like – then it is essential to read all the questions so you can eliminate the two that are most difficult. If, however, you are asked to answer all the questions, there may be danger in trying to answer the easiest one first because you may find that you will spend too much time on it. The best technique is to answer the first question, then proceed to the second, etc.

5) Time your answers. Before the exam begins, write down the time it started, then add the time allowed for the examination and write down the time it must be completed, then divide the time available somewhat as follows:
   - If 3-1/2 hours are allowed, that would be 210 minutes. If you have 80 objective-type questions, that would be an average of 2-1/2 minutes per question. Allow yourself no more than 2 minutes per question, or a total of 160 minutes, which will permit about 50 minutes to review.
   - If for the time allotment of 210 minutes there are 7 essay questions to answer, that would average about 30 minutes a question. Give yourself only 25 minutes per question so that you have about 35 minutes to review.

6) The most important instruction is to *read each question* and make sure you know what is wanted. The second most important instruction is to *time yourself properly* so that you answer every question. The third most important instruction is to *answer every question*. Guess if you have to but include something for each question. Remember that you will receive no credit for a blank and will probably receive some credit if you write something in answer to an essay question. If you guess a letter – say "B" for a multiple-choice question – you may have guessed right. If you leave a blank as an answer to a multiple-choice question, the examiners may respect your feelings but it will not add a point to your score. Some exams may penalize you for wrong answers, so in such cases *only*, you may not want to guess unless you have some basis for your answer.

7) Suggestions
   a. Objective-type questions
      1. Examine the question booklet for proper sequence of pages and questions
      2. Read all instructions carefully
      3. Skip any question which seems too difficult; return to it after all other questions have been answered
      4. Apportion your time properly; do not spend too much time on any single question or group of questions
      5. Note and underline key words – *all, most, fewest, least, best, worst, same, opposite,* etc.
      6. Pay particular attention to negatives
      7. Note unusual option, e.g., unduly long, short, complex, different or similar in content to the body of the question
      8. Observe the use of "hedging" words – *probably, may, most likely,* etc.
      9. Make sure that your answer is put next to the same number as the question
      10. Do not second-guess unless you have good reason to believe the second answer is definitely more correct
      11. Cross out original answer if you decide another answer is more accurate; do not erase until you are ready to hand your paper in
      12. Answer all questions; guess unless instructed otherwise
      13. Leave time for review

   b. Essay questions
      1. Read each question carefully
      2. Determine exactly what is wanted. Underline key words or phrases.
      3. Decide on outline or paragraph answer
      4. Include many different points and elements unless asked to develop any one or two points or elements
      5. Show impartiality by giving pros and cons unless directed to select one side only
      6. Make and write down any assumptions you find necessary to answer the questions
      7. Watch your English, grammar, punctuation and choice of words
      8. Time your answers; don't crowd material

8) Answering the essay question

Most essay questions can be answered by framing the specific response around several key words or ideas. Here are a few such key words or ideas:

M's: manpower, materials, methods, money, management
P's: purpose, program, policy, plan, procedure, practice, problems, pitfalls, personnel, public relations
   a. Six basic steps in handling problems:
      1. Preliminary plan and background development
      2. Collect information, data and facts
      3. Analyze and interpret information, data and facts
      4. Analyze and develop solutions as well as make recommendations

5. Prepare report and sell recommendations
6. Install recommendations and follow up effectiveness

b. Pitfalls to avoid
1. *Taking things for granted* – A statement of the situation does not necessarily imply that each of the elements is necessarily true; for example, a complaint may be invalid and biased so that all that can be taken for granted is that a complaint has been registered
2. *Considering only one side of a situation* – Wherever possible, indicate several alternatives and then point out the reasons you selected the best one
3. *Failing to indicate follow up* – Whenever your answer indicates action on your part, make certain that you will take proper follow-up action to see how successful your recommendations, procedures or actions turn out to be
4. *Taking too long in answering any single question* – Remember to time your answers properly

EXAMINATION SECTION

EXAMINATION SECTION
TEST 1

DIRECTIONS: Each drawing below is followed by a list of five possible names. Select the name that corresponds to the object drawn. *PRINT THE LETTER OF THE CORRECT ANSWER IN THE SPACE AT THE RIGHT.*

1._____

1.

A. Carpenters square   B. Level
C. Wooden rule   D. Folding rule
E. Steel tape

2._____

2.

A. Finish nail   B. Common nail
C. Casing nail   D. Box nail
E. Roofing nail

3._____

3.

A. Level   B. Combination rule
C. Steel rule   D. Zig-zag rule
E. Flexible steel rule

4._____

4.

A. Firmer chisel   B. Cold chisel
C. Tang chisel   D. Socket chisel
E. Bevel chisel

1

5.

A. Bevel   B. Chamfer   C. Angle
D. Corner bevel   E. Check

5.____

6.

A. Dado joint   B. Rabbet joint
C. Mortise and tenon   D. Dowel joint
E. Lap joint

6.____

7.

A. Keyhole saw   B. Compass saw
C. Coping saw   D. Combination saw
E. Back saw

7.____

8.

A. Jointer plane   B. Block plane
C. Rabbet plane   D. Fore plane
E. Smooth plane

8.____

9.

A. Marking gauge
B. Protractor
C. Bevel protractor
D. Sliding T bevel
E. Draw knife

10.

A. Scribe
B. Caliper
C. Awl
D. Burnisher
E. Leather punch

11.

A. Rip saw teeth
B. Saw kerf
C. Crosscut saw teeth
D. Back saw teeth
E. Combination saw teeth

12.

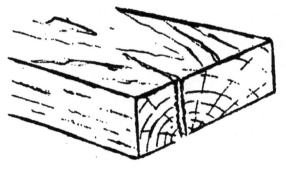

A. Check   B. Knot   C. Decay   D. Kerf   E. Spike

13.

13.____

    A.   Twist drill   B.   Gimlet bit
    C.   Iron drill   D.   Auger bit
    E.   Automatic drill bit

14.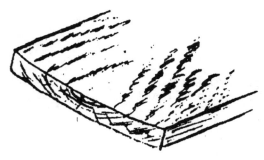

14.____

    A. Wind   B. Twist   C. Warp   D. Shrink   E. Curve

15.

15.____

    A.   Bar clamp   B.   Cabinet clamp   C.   Hand clamp
    D.   Spring clamp   E.   C clamp

16.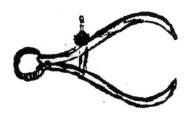

16.____

    A.   Caliper   B.   Compass   C.   Divider
    D.   Micrometer   E.   Vernier caliper

17.

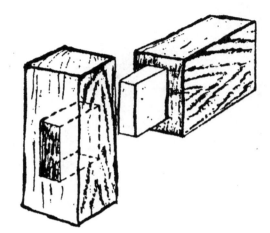

A. Lap joint   B. Dowel joint
C. Stud joint   D. Mortise and tenon
E. Rail joint

17._____

18.

A. Burnisher   B. Dowel pointer
C. Doweling jig   D. Nail set
E. Depth gauge

18._____

19.

A. Countersink   B. Counterbore   C. Auger bit
D. Live center   E. Spur center

19._____

20.

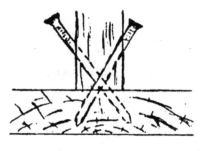

A. Dovetailing   B. Toenailing   C. Rabbeting
D. Clenching   E. Setting

20._____

21.____

21.

- A. Gimlet bit
- B. Iron drill
- C. Combination wood drill and countersink
- D. Counterbore wood bit
- E. Phillips screw drill

22.____

22.

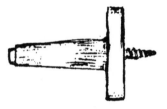

- A. Sanding block
- C. Regulator
- E. Stuffing tool
- B. Push stick
- D. Webbing stretcher

23.____

23.

- A. Screw center
- C. Dead center
- E. Friction plate
- B. Live center
- D. Faceplate

24.____

24.

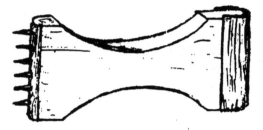

- A. Forstner bit
- D. Plug cutter
- B. Dowel pointer
- E. Micro drill
- C. Counterbore

25.____

25.

- A. Vernier caliper
- C. Outside caliper
- E. Hermaphrodite caliper
- B. Micrometer
- D. Inside caliper

KEY (CORRECT ANSWERS)

1.	D	11.	A
2.	C	12.	A
3.	E	13.	E
4.	C	14.	C
5.	B	15.	E
6.	E	16.	A
7.	E	17.	D
8.	B	18.	B
9.	D	19.	A
10.	C	20.	B

21.	C
22.	D
23.	A
24.	D
25.	E

TEST 2

DIRECTIONS: Each question or incomplete statement is followed by several suggested answers or completions. Select the one that BEST answers the question or completes the statement. *PRINT THE LETTER OF THE CORRECT ANSWER IN THE SPACE AT THE RIGHT.*

1. The handsaw with chisel-like teeth is the _____ saw.

    A. crosscut   B. back   C. rip
    D. coping   E. dovetail

1.____

2. A board foot is a piece of lumber

    A. 12 x 1 x 1   B. 12 x 12 x 12   C. 1 x 12 x 1
    D. 1 x 12 x 12   E. 6 x 12 x 1

2.____

3. The SMALLEST division of measurement on most measuring instruments in woodworking is

    A. halves   B. sixteenths   C. quarters
    D. eighths   E. thirty-seconds

3.____

4. A jig used for boring dowel-rod holes is the

    A. dowel pointer   B. zig-zag jig
    C. auger bit jig   D. doweling jig
    E. counterbore

4.____

5. Lumber prices are GENERALLY quoted by the hardwood lumber industry in board foot amounts of

    A. 100   B. 10   C. 1   D. 300   E. 1000

5.____

6. The handsaw to use when MOST accuracy is desired is the _____ saw.

    A. rip   B. back   C. crosscut   D. coping   E. compass

6.____

7. The CORRECT tool for cleaning the teeth on files is the

    A. file card   B. knife   C. steel wool
    D. surform tool   E. file set

7.____

8. The screw hole which accompanies the screw threads is the _____ hole.

    A. shank   B. counter   C. tapping
    D. clearance   E. pilot

8.____

9. The HIGHEST grade of hardwood lumber is referred to as

    A. select   B. #1 common   C. firsts
    D. wormy   E. shop

9.____

10. A good thinner for paints, varnishes, and enamels is

    A. lacquer thinner   B. turpentine
    C. alcohol   D. shellac
    E. Japan drier

10.____

11. Which of the following refers to the drying of lumber?   11._____

    A. LD   B. S2S   C. Quartered D. M   E. KD

12. The MOST important thing to consider when planning a project is   12._____

    A. finish
    B. design of the project
    C. type of construction
    D. kinds of joints
    E. whether there is a need for the article

13. Auger bit sizes are graduated in   13._____

    A. fourths   B. eighths   C. twelfths
    D. sixteenths   E. thirty-seconds

14. Which of the following woods is an open-grained wood?   14._____

    A. Mahogany   B. Maple   C. Redwood
    D. Pine   E. Cedar

15. The size of the bandsaw is determined by the   15._____

    A. diameter of the wheels
    B. width of the blade
    C. length of the blade
    D. distance from the blade to the overarm
    E. shortest possible radius it will cut

16. The machine to use when cutting out an inside area is the   16._____

    A. bandsaw   B. circular saw   C. jig saw
    D. radial arm saw   E. jointer

17. Which of the following is NOT an advantage of plywood?   17._____

    A. Fewer glue joints necessary
    B. Resistance to warp and wind
    C. Requires less sanding and surface preparation
    D. Edge preparation is non-existent
    E. Easy to store

18. The MAIN advantage of an oil finish over a surface finish is   18._____

    A. high gloss
    B. ability to resist dents and cuts
    C. ability to resist dust nibbs
    D. ability to take wax
    E. ease of refinishing

19. The drawing MOST used in project planning is the   19._____

    A. cavalier   B. working drawing
    C. oblique   D. architectural drawing
    E. draft drawing

20. The key to success in woodworking is — 20._____

    A. sharp tools
    B. large work area
    C. well-planned project drawings
    D. good materials
    E. clean shop

21. The tool to use for rough turning on the lathe is the — 21._____

    A. skew   B. spearpoint   C. parting tool
    D. round nose   E. gouge

22. The size of the jointer is determined by the — 22._____

    A. length of the fence
    B. maximum depth of cut
    C. length of the blades
    D. length of front table
    E. diameter of spindle

23. The BEST joint to use when making a simple table with legs and rails is the — 23._____

    A. dado   B. mortise and tenon
    C. butt   D. lap
    E. miter

24. Which of the following is NOT produced from wood? — 24._____

    A. Rubber   B. Paper   C. Rayon
    D. Imitation leather   E. Porcelain

25. Lumber for furniture construction should have a moisture content of — 25._____

    A. 6-10 percent   B. 2-5 percent   C. 10-15 percent
    D. 20-30 percent   E. zero

KEY (CORRECT ANSWERS)

1.	C	11.	E
2.	D	12.	E
3.	B	13.	D
4.	D	14.	A
5.	E	15.	A
6.	B	16.	C
7.	A	17.	D
8.	E	18.	E
9.	C	19.	B
10.	B	20.	A

21.	E
22.	C
23.	B
24.	E
25.	A

———

EXAMINATION SECTION
TEST 1

DIRECTIONS: Each question shows a drawing that is followed by several suggested names of the object drawn. Select the name that correctly identifies the object. *PRINT THE LETTER OF THE CORRECT ANSWER IN THE SPACE AT THE RIGHT.*

1.

   A. Casing nail   B. Flooring nail
   C. Finishing nail   D. Common nail
   E. Brad

1.___

2.

   A. Bar clamp   B. Hand screw clamp
   C. C clamp   D. Speed clamp
   E. Spring clamp

2.___

3.

   A. Foerstner bit   B. Twist drill
   C. Speed bit   D. Expansive bit
   E. Auger bit

3.___

4.

   A. Dividers   B. Compass   C. Trammel points
   D. Bow compass   E. None of the above

4.___

5.

5.____

A. Socket chisel
D. Gouge chisel
B. Cold chisel
E. None of the above
C. Tang chisel

6.

6.____

A. Crosscut saw
D. Scroll saw
B. Compass saw
E. Jig saw
C. Coping saw

7.

7.____

A. Try square
C. Framing square
E. Steel square
B. Tee square
D. Combination square

8.

8.____

A. Backsaw
D. Coping saw
B. Crosscut saw
E. Compass saw
C. Keyhole saw

9.

9.____

A. Sliding T bevel
D. Tee square
B. Spokeshave
E. None of the above
C. Bevel protractor

10.

    A. Spokeshave   B. Surface form   C. Bevel knife
    D. Draw knife   E. Jack knife

10.____

11.

    A. Drill press   B. Breast drill   C. Hand drill
    D. Brace   E. Automatic drill

11.____

12.

    A. Cabinet scraper   B. Hand scraper
    C. Plane iron cap   D. Hand chisel
    E. Plane iron

12.____

13.

    A. Try square   B. Combination square
    C. Framing square   D. Level
    E. Marking gauge

13.____

14.

    A. Skew   B. Gouge   C. Diamond point
    D. Spear point   E. Parting tool

14.____

15.

A. Punch
D. Chisel
B. Countersink
E. None of the above
C. Nail set

15.____

16.

A. Countersink
C. Screw-mate counterbore
E. None of the above
B. Counterbore
D. Speed drill

16.____

17.

A. Rabbet joint
C. Mortise and tenon
E. Miter joint
B. Dado joint
D. Butt joint

17.____

18.

A. Dado   B. Rabbet   C. Mortise   D. Lap   E. Miter

18.____

19.

When planing or surfacing, one should work in which direction?

A. ⟵   B. ⟶   C. ⟶
D. All of the above   E. None of the above

19.____

20.

20.____

A. End lap joint   B. Half lap joint
C. Middle lap   D. Cross lap
E. None of the above

21.

21.____

A. Chamfer B. Taper C. Rabbet D. Dado E. Bevel

22.

22.____

A. Drill bit gauge   B. Doweling jig
C. Dowel drill guide   D. Auger bit
E. None of the above

23.____

23.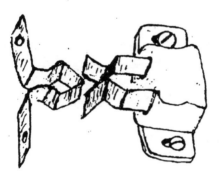

A. Friction catch   B. Magnetic catch
C. Elbow catch   D. Ball catch
E. Slide catch

24.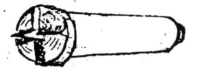

24.____

A. Dead center B. Screw center C. Ball center
D. Live center   E. Hard center

25.

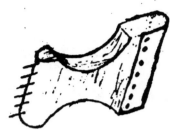

25.____

A. Burnisher
D. Sanding block

B. Hand router
E. Lapping tool

C. Webbing stretcher

_____

KEY (CORRECT ANSWERS)

1.	D		11.	C
2.	B		12.	E
3.	E		13.	B
4.	A		14.	E
5.	A		15.	C
6.	B		16.	A
7.	A		17.	A
8.	D		18.	A
9.	A		19.	A
10.	D		20.	A

21.	E
22.	E
23.	A
24.	D
25.	C

_____

TEST 2

DIRECTIONS: Each question or incomplete statement is followed by several suggested answers or completions. Select the one that BEST answers the question or completes the statement. *PRINT THE LETTER OF THE CORRECT ANSWER IN THE SPACE AT THE RIGHT.*

1. The MOST important fundamental in woodworking, according to many authorities, is   1.____

    A.   the attitude of the workman toward his work
    B.   the equipment available
    C.   the time spent executing the processes
    D.   sharp cutting edges
    E.   the quality of material used

2. When cutting wood or lumber straight across the grain, the handsaw used should be the   2.____
    _____ saw.

    A.   rip   B.   band   C.   compass
    D.   crosscut   E.   coping

3. Dressed lumber is smaller than the actual quoted size; for example, a finished one inch   3.____
    walnut board would measure _____ inch.

    A.   5/16   B.   13/16   C.   7/16   D.   9/32   E.   1/16

4. The characteristic found in lumber and considered not to be a defect is   4.____

    A.   check   B.   decay   C.   knots
    D.   split ends   E.   grain

5. Lumber is purchased by the   5.____

    A.   foot   B.   square foot   C.   board yard
    D.   board foot   E.   square yard

6. A bill of woodworking materials would NOT include the   6.____

    A.   lumber   B.   plywood
    C.   hardware   D.   finishing materials
    E.   drawing of project

7. In woodworking, the four MOST common portable electric tools are the   7.____

    A.   jig saw, router, drill press, and sander
    B.   grinder, router, drill, and saber saw
    C.   electric hand drill, router, saber saw, and sander
    D.   jig saw, hand drill, chisel, and band saw
    E.   none of the above

8. For general cutting of wood with the saber saw, the number of teeth per inch the blade   8.____
    should have are

    A.   4   B.   7   C.   20   D.   12   E.   17

9. The INCORRECT method of transferring a pattern to stock is 9.____

    A. tracing the pattern with carbon paper
    B. making a metal template
    C. enlarging the design directly on the stock
    D. cutting out the pattern to use for tracing
    E. making a plywood template

10. The joint used PRIMARILY to install shelves, partitions, or steps in bookcases, etc. is the _____ joint. 10.____

    A. miter   B. rabbet   C. lap   D. dado   E. butt

11. When sanding by hand, the size of paper that should be selected is _____ inches. 11.____

    A. 6 x 11   B. 8 x 11   C. 10 x 12
    D. 9 x 11   E. 9 x 12

12. If a shop has radial and circular saws, the MOST common use of the radial saw should be 12.____

    A. ripping   B. mitering
    C. routing   D. cutting stock to length
    E. cutting dados

13. 6-d refers to the size of 13.____

    A. screws   B. clawhammers   C. screw eyes
    D. saws   E. nails

14. The board that will safely hold up the GREATEST weight is 14.____

    A. 1" x 6" on edge   B. 2" x 4" on flat side
    C. 2" x 6" on flat side   D. 4" x 6" on edge
    E. 2" x 8" on edge

15. The wood considered to be the FINEST American furniture wood is 15.____

    A. black walnut   B. cherry   C. birch
    D. pine   E. red gum

16. The MAIN purpose of sanding with number 400-wet or dry abrasive papers is to 16.____

    A. rough the surface between coats of finish
    B. remove dust nibbs
    C. polish
    D. clean surfaces
    E. apply wax

17. One of the characteristics of wood which any woodworker, to be successful, MUST keep constantly in mind is that 17.____

    A. wood is stronger in its length
    B. wood expands and contracts in its width
    C. wood is easily bent and molded
    D. wood is easier to cut across grain than with the grain
    E. wood must always be protected from water

18. One of the MOST dangerous operations executed on the table saw is the   18.____

    A. cutting stock to narrow widths
    B. crosscutting
    C. dadoing
    D. cutting of duplicate pieces between the rip fence and the saw blade
    E. tenoning

19. The MOST appropriate instrument to use in making an odd angle is   19.____

    A. T-bevel   B. try-square   C. dividers
    D. marking gauge   E. spirit level

20. When doing work on the jointer, a push-block should also be used if the stock is less than _____ inches.   20.____

    A. 18   B. 16   C. 12   D. 20   E. 24

21. The bevel of the plane-iron should be _____ degrees.   21.____

    A. 10 to 15   B. 12 to 20   C. 25 to 30
    D. 40 to 45   E. 60 to 65

22. The depth of a cut of the jointer as a rule should NEVER be more than _____ inch.   22.____

    A. 1/2   B. 3/8   C. 1/4   D. 1/8   E. 1/16

23. The operation that cannot be performed on the drill press is   23.____

    A. routing   B. shaping   C. drilling
    D. mortising   E. turning

24. A 6-d nail is _____ inch(es) long.   24.____

    A. 2   B. 3   C. 4   D. 5   E. 1

25. The MOST used joint in drawer construction is the   25.____

    A. dado   B. rabbet   C. dovetail
    D. dowel   E. butt

KEY (CORRECT ANSWERS)

1.	D	11.	D
2.	D	12.	D
3.	B	13.	E
4.	E	14.	D
5.	D	15.	A
6.	E	16.	A
7.	C	17.	B
8.	B	18.	D
9.	C	19.	A
10.	D	20.	C

21.	C
22.	D
23.	E
24.	A
25.	B

———

EXAMINATION SECTION
TEST 1

DIRECTIONS: Each question or incomplete statement is followed by several suggested answers or completions. Select the one that BEST answers the question or completes the statement. *PRINT THE LETTER OF THE CORRECT ANSWER IN THE SPACE AT THE RIGHT.*

1. Hollow columns and posts made at the mill are frequently kerfed on the back to   1.____

    A. allow drainage   B. prevent warping
    C. reduce weight   D. have air passage

2. Work benches should be made of   2.____

    A. quartered oak   B. sycamore
    C. silver maple   D. rock maple

3. The upright side members of a door are called   3.____

    A. rails   B. stiles   C. panels   D. mullions

4. The standard height of a dining room table is   4.____

    A. 24"   B. 30"   C. 36"   D. 20"

5. In what order should the dimensions of stock in a bill of material be listed?   5.____

    A. Length, width, thickness
    B. Thickness, width, length
    C. Width, length, thickness
    D. Length, thickness, width

6. A square cut across the middle of a board from edge to edge is called a   6.____

    A. rabbet   B. groove   C. dado   D. gain

7. A circular saw is used to   7.____

    A. saw out curved shapes
    B. cut slices from cylindrical forms
    C. rip or crosscut lumber
    D. cut mortises

8. A panel is _____ into a frame.   8.____

    A. glued   B. just grooved   C. nailed   D. doweled

9. A burnisher is used to condition   9.____

    A. saws   B. chisels   C. scrapers   D. knives

10. Stock is roughed off and made cylindrical on the wood- ! worker's lathe with the   10.____

    A. gauge   B. parting tool
    C. skew chisel   D. round nose chisel

24. Rift sawn pine flooring is also called   24.____

    A. comb grain   B. flitch
    C. slash sawn   D. waney

25. The horizontal member on top of the studs or wall to which the rafters are framed is   25.____
called a

    A. ribbon   B. plate
    C. frieze   D. ridge-pole

26. Any line on a rafter that is vertical when the rafter is in its proper position is called   26.____

    A. cutting line   B. plumb line
    C. cut of the roof   D. seat line

27. Greater strength in a building is obtained if the sheathing is run   27.____

    A. vertically   B. diagonally
    C. horizontally   D. lapped

28. The rise of a common rafter divided by the span of the building equals the _____ of the   28.____
roof.

    A. grade   B. slope   C. pitch   D. run

29. In a stairway there is one less tread than there are   29.____

    A. risers   B. balusters   C. stringers   D. nosings

30. The length of an 8d common nail is _____ inches.   30.____

    A. 2   B. 2 1/4   C. 2 3/16   D. 2 1/2

31. The nails ordinarily used to nail down 7/8 inch rough flooring boards are _____ penny   31.____
commons.

    A. 8   B. 12   C. 16   D. 4

32. Pitch of roof is the ratio of   32.____

    A. *rise* to *run* of rafter   B. *rise* to length of rafter
    C. *rise* to span of roof   D. *run* to length of rafter

33. The blade is held at a very low angle, the bevel is on the upper side, and there is no cap   33.____
iron in the _____ plane.

    A. block   B. jointer   C. smooth   D. fore

34. The gauge that is used for locating lines for door hinges is the _____ gauge.   34.____

    A. mortise   B. marking   C. finger   D. butt

35. The tool used to make the hole for the head of a flat head wood screw is called a   35.____

    A. gimlet   B. reamer
    C. punch   D. countersink

47. Varnish is USUALLY rubbed down with 47._____

    A. emery dust   B. pumice
    C. graphite   D. chalk

48. Shellac is thinned with 48._____

    A. alcohol   B. turpentine
    C. water   D. linseed oil

49. One of the CHIEF disadvantages of water stain is that it 49._____

    A. does not penetrate as deeply as an oil stain
    B. raises the grain of the wood
    C. fades readily
    D. has a dull appearance when it dries

50. Creosote is impregnated in wood to 50._____

    A. stain the surface
    B. prevent decay
    C. give a smooth oily surface
    D. give a hard protective surface

KEY (CORRECT ANSWERS)

1. B	11. B	21. A	31. A	41. A
2. D	12. C	22. A	32. C	42. C
3. B	13. A	23. C	33. A	43. D
4. B	14. D	24. A	34. D	44. A
5. B	15. C	25. B	35. D	45. B
6. C	16. B	26. B	36. C	46. C
7. C	17. B	27. B	37. B	47. B
8. B	18. B	28. C	38. D	48. A
9. C	19. C	29. A	39. A	49. B
10. A	20. B	30. D	40. C	50. B

11. The BEST single criterion to evaluate the strength of different pieces of wood of the same species is the   11.____

    A.   relation of summer wood to spring wood
    B.   weight
    C.   moisture content
    D.   number of rings per inch

12. Which of the following woods is MOST commonly used for core stock of plywood?   12.____

    A.   Oak   B.   Maple   C.   Poplar   D.   Pine

13. Dowels are USUALLY made of   13.____

    A.   birch   B.   maple   C.   hickory   D.   oak

14. The wood that was popularized by Chippendale was   14.____

    A.   mahogany   B.   maple   C.   cherry   D.   walnut

15. The cheapest of veneers are produced by   15.____

    A.   rotary cutting   B.   slicing
    C.   sawing   D.   splitting

16. When several boards are joined edge to edge to make a wide surface,   16.____

    A.   the rings of adjoining boards should be reversed
    B.   the boards should be securely screwed down
    C.   a water-resisting glue should be used
    D.   dowels should be used

17. The abbreviation *S2S* means   17.____

    A.   surface two sides   B.   sand two surfaces
    C.   square two sides   D.   secure two sets

18. To true a board *in wind,* plane   18.____

    A.   across the grain
    B.   diagonally from one high corner to the other
    C.   with the grain
    D.   diagonally from one low corner to the other

19. Medullary rays are VERY pronounced in   19.____

    A.   apple wood   B.   rift sawn cedar
    C.   quarter-sawn oak   D.   random width yellow pine

20. Wood filler should be used on   20.____

    A.   maple   B.   birch   C.   oak   D.   poplar

21. A wood much used for white inlay is   21.____

    A.   white pine   B.   holly
    C.   gumwood   D.   rosewood

33. In gumming a circular saw, we   33._____

    A. bind a piece of wood between the saw and the fence
    B. grind out the gullets
    C. apply gum arable to increase cutting efficiency
    D. increase set of the teeth

34. A square of roofing material covers _____ sq.ft.   34._____

    A. 63   B. 100   C. 144   D. 125

35. What size nails would be BEST to nail two 2 x 6's together when the nails are to be clinched?   35._____

    A. 8-D   B. 10-D   C. 12-D   D. 16-D

36. To bore a 1/2" hole in a board, a #_____ auger bit should be used.   36._____

    A. 5   B. 1/2   C. 6   D. 8

37. A jack plane is _____ long.   37._____

    A. 6"   B. 9"   C. 14"   D. 18"

38. The teeth of the back saw are similar in shape to a   38._____

    A. coping saw   B. crosscut saw
    C. ripsaw   D. band saw

39. A scraper should be used   39._____

    A. after planing to secure a smoother finish
    B. before planing to remove mill marks
    C. after sanding to remove sandpaper scratches
    D. to smooth a varnish finish

40. The frog is a part of the   40._____

    A. brace   B. plane
    C. marking gauge   D. mitre box

41. The tool MOST frequently used for planing curves is a   41._____

    A. circular plane   B. spokeshave
    C. block plane   D. core box plane

42. A finish cut without planing or sanding may be accomplished with the _____ saw.   42._____

    A. rip circular   B. cross-cut circular
    C. combination circular D. gang

43. The glue which is MOST nearly waterproof is   43._____

    A. hide   B. fish
    C. casein   D. phenol resin

KEY (CORRECT ANSWERS)

1.	C	11.	B	21.	B	31.	A	41.	C
2.	B	12.	C	22.	B	32.	B	42.	C
3.	C	13.	B	23.	B	33.	B	43.	A
4.	B	14.	A	24.	B	34.	B	44.	D
5.	B	15.	A	25.	A	35.	D	45.	D
6.	C	16.	A	26.	D	36.	D	46.	A
7.	B	17.	A	27.	C	37.	C	47.	B
8.	A	18.	A	28.	A	38.	B	48.	C
9.	A	19.	B	29.	C	39.	A	49.	D
10.	B	20.	B	30.	D	40.	D	50.	D

EXAMINATION SECTION
TEST 1

DIRECTIONS: Each question or incomplete statement is followed by several suggested answers or completions. Select the one that BEST answers the question or completes the statement. *PRINT THE LETTER OF THE CORRECT ANSWER IN THE SPACE AT THE RIGHT.*

1. The order in which the dimensions of stock are listed on a bill of materials is   1.____

   A. thickness, length, and width
   B. thickness, width, and length
   C. width, length, and thickness
   D. length, thickness, and width

2. The gauge number range for a 1" F.H.S. wood screw is   2.____

   A. 6 to 14   B. 2 to 12   C. 4 to 10   D. 6 to 16

3. The glue that will BEST withstand extreme exposure to moisture and water is _____   3.____
   glue.

   A. polyvinyl   B. resorcinol
   C. powdered resin   D. protein

4. Four board feet of lumber, listed at $350.00 per M, will cost   4.____

   A. $3.50   B. $1.40   C. $1.80   D. $4.00

5. The cap iron or chip breaker stiffens the plane iron and   5.____

   A. protects the cutting edge
   B. curls the shaving
   C. regulates the thickness of the shaving
   D. reduces mouth gap

6. The standard minimum weight per square foot for single strength window glass that is   6.____
   manufactured in the United States is _____ ounces.

   A. 8   B. 12   C. 16   D. 19

7. Coping-saw blades have teeth shaped like those on a _____ saw.   7.____

   A. dovetail   B. crosscut   C. back   D. rip

8. Of the following, the claw hammer that is BEST suited for general use in an industrial arts   8.____
   woodworking shop is the _____ claw.

   A. straight   B. bell-faced curved
   C. plain-faced curved   D. adze eye curved

9. The hole size for the shank or body of a 1 1/2" #10 R.H. Blued wood screw is   9.____

   A. 11/64   B. 3/16   C. 13/64   D. 7/32

10. The standard length of a 3/8" dowel rod is _____ ft.   10.____

   A. 1   B. 2   C. 3   D. 4

11. The natural binder which cements wood fibers together and makes wood solid is   11.___

    A. cellulose   B. lignin
    C. alpha-cellulose   D. trichocarpa

12. The plane that is BEST suited for trimming the bottom of a dado or lap joint is the _____   12.___
plane.

    A. block   B. router   C. rabbet   D. core-box

13. The trim around doors and windows is referred to as the   13.___

    A. facia   B. plancier   C. casing   D. jamb

14. Hardboard was discovered accidentally by   14.___

    A. Franklin A. Masonite   B. George S. Benton
    C. Joseph B. Mersereau   D. William H. Mason

15. The width of a saw kerf is affected by the   15.___

    A. fleam   B. hook   C. bevel   D. set

16. The drying process of spirit stains, dissolved with alcohol, may be slowed down consider-   16.___
ably by adding a small amount of

    A. naphtha   B. zinc chloride
    C. ammonium chloride   D. ochre

17. Brads are fasteners that are similar to _____ nails.   17.___

    A. escutcheon   B. box
    C. finishing   D. duplex head

18. The plane in which the plane iron is inserted with its bevel in the up position is the   18.___
_____ plane.

    A. fore   B. rabbet   C. block   D. circular

19. Trammel points are used to   19.___

    A. set the stadia rod
    B. lay out large arcs and circles
    C. determine the slope for stair stringers
    D. maintain the horizontal line when laying bricks

20. Of the following, the inch division that does NOT appear on the steel square used for the   20.___
layout of rafters is

    A. hundredths   B. sixty-fourths
    C. sixteenths   D. eighths

21. Of the following, the exterior paint that is LEAST likely to discolor when exposed to indus-   21.___
trial gases or fumes is

    A. T.L.Z.   B. T.Z.   C. L   D. L.Z.

22. Coating materials used to protect wood against fire usually contain a water soluble fire-retardant such as   22._____

    A. ammonium chloride   B. sodium perborate
    C. sodium silicate   D. sal soda

23. Of the following, the wood that has pores large enough to take wood filler effectively when desired but small enough, as a rule, to be painted satisfactorily without filling is   23._____

    A. ash   B. hickory   C. birch   D. maple

24. The file used for filing saw teeth with an angle of less than 60° is known as the _____ file.   24._____

    A. slim taper   B. cant
    C. taper   D. XF

25. The stock that is BEST suited for fence posts is   25._____

    A. Sitka spruce   B. cypress
    C. Douglas fir   D. long leaf yellow pine

26. The uppermost horizontal member of a framed wall is the   26._____

    A. shoe   B. purlin   C. sleeper   D. plate

27. The common nail BEST suited to face-nail a sole plate to joists 16" on center is the _____ d.   27._____

    A. 8   B. 10   C. 12   D. 16

28. The auger bit that is LEAST likely to bind when boring stock that has a considerable amount of pitch is   28._____

    A. solid center   B. single twist
    C. double twist   D. double spur

29. The dovetail lock joint is a(n)   29._____

    A. half blind dovetail used in drawer construction on better furniture
    B. through multiple dovetail used as a corner joint in cabinet construction
    C. invisible mitred dovetail joint
    D. means of reinforcing two units joined together with a simple butt joint

30. Medium garnet paper is designated as follows: 80-D-(0). The letter D refers to the   30._____

    A. type of mesh used to determine grit size
    B. size of grit
    C. weight of paper stock used for backing
    D. resin bond and resin size

KEY (CORRECT ANSWERS)

1.	B		16.	A
2.	A		17.	C
3.	B		18.	C
4.	B		19.	B
5.	B		20.	B
6.	D		21.	B
7.	D		22.	C
8.	B		23.	C
9.	B		24.	B
10.	C		25.	B
11.	B		26.	D
12.	B		27.	D
13.	C		28.	B
14.	D		29.	D
15.	D		30.	C

TEST 2

DIRECTIONS: Each question or incomplete statement is followed by several suggested answers or completions. Select the one that BEST answers the question or completes the statement. *PRINT THE LETTER OF THE CORRECT ANSWER IN THE SPACE AT THE RIGHT.*

1 A wash solution of shellac usually consists of _____ part(s) of 4 lb. cut shellac to _____ parts of alcohol.

    A. 1; 3   B. 1; 7   C. 2; 2   D. 2; 6

1.____

2. The bristles of a camel's-hair brush are obtained from the tails of

    A. China hogs   B. camels
    C. Russian squirrels   D. rabbits

2.____

3. Spar varnish is tough, hard, elastic, highly resistant to dampness and is classified as a _____ varnish.

    A. medium oil   B. base oil
    C. ester gum   D. long oil

3.____

4. When cutting double thickness glass, the BEST lubricant to use in conjunction with the glass cutter is

    A. kerosene   B. varnolene   C. benzine   D. turpentine

4.____

5. In a piece of 5-ply veneer, the layer under the face veneer is known as the

    A. core   B. lattice core
    C. face banding   D. crossbands

5.____

6. Grozing is the process of

    A. glazing with ground colors in oil
    B. chipping glass
    C. staining over an undercoat
    D. highlighting a stained finish

6.____

7. The points of nails or brads are sometimes blunted to

    A. avoid splitting of stock
    B. reduce fibre crushing
    C. increase holding power
    D. increase withdrawal resistance

7.____

8. The type of frame structure that does NOT have a break at the intervening floor line is known as

    A. braced   B. platform   C. balloon   D. western

8.____

9. When preparing a plane iron for general purpose planing, the cutting edge of the plane iron should be

    A. slightly convex
    B. straight with slightly rounded corners
    C. straight and square
    D. crowned

9.____

10. The plane BEST suited for smoothing the bottom of a dado is the _____ plane.   10.__

    A.   rabbet   B.   filister   C.   bull-nose   D.   router

11. In frame construction, the ledger board is used to support the   11.__

    A.   studs   B.   headers   C.   joists   D.   plate

12. The number of teeth per inch on a 10" backsaw ranges from   12.__

    A.   8 to 12   B.   12 to 16   C.   16 to 20   D.   20 to 24

13. Cross-grained wood can BEST be smoothed with a   13.__

    A.   smooth plane   B.   cabinet scraper
    C.   fore plane   D.   block plane

14. The number stamped on the shank of a gimlet indicates the size in _____ of an inch.   14.__

    A.   sixty-fourths   B.   forty-eighths
    C.   thirty-seconds   D.   sixteenths

15. Oil is used on an oil stone during a whetting operation to lubricate and   15.__

    A.   accelerate the sharpening
    B.   prevent steel particles from loading the stone
    C.   regulate whetting
    D.   cool the blade to prevent loss of temper

16. To produce a true plane (work face) on a board that is in wind, it is advisable to plane   16.__

    A.   across the grain edge to the edge
    B.   along the grain end to the end
    C.   diagonally from one high corner to the other
    D.   one corner at a time

17. Marquetry is a form of wood   17.__

    A.   applique   B.   carving   C.   inlaying   D.   joinery

18. When fastening two pieces of wood together with screws, the pilot hole should be _____ of the screw.   18.__

    A.   the size of the threaded part
    B.   the size of the root diameter
    C.   slightly smaller than the shank
    D.   slightly larger than the shank

19. Of the following, the solvent that should NOT be used to thin a copal varnish is   19.__

    A.   benzene   B.   varnolene
    C.   turpentine   D.   alcohol

20. The point on a foerstener bit has a _____ lead.   20.__

    A.   fine   B.   medium   C.   coarse   D.   no

21. The MOST suitable joint for joining the top rail to the stile of a panel door is the   21._____

    A. stub mortise and tenon
    B. haunched mortise and tenon
    C. locked dowel
    D. tongue and groove

22. A board 3/4" x 10" x 10', if purchased at 30¢ a board foot instead of at 30¢ a linear foot, will cost   22._____

    A. 60 cents more   B. 45 cents more
    C. the same   D. 50 cents less

23. In dimensioned lumber, the size of a 2" x 4" is   23._____

    A. 1 1/2" x 3 1/2"   B. 1 5/8" x 3 5/8"
    C. 1 3/4" x 3 3/4"   D. 2" x 4"

24. The vertical member which separates 2 or more adjacent windows is known as the   24._____

    A. muntin   B. meeting rail
    C. mullion   D. yoke

25. One of the new developments in the lumber industry is the manufacture of stock for studs, jambs, door stock, etc. through   25._____

    A. selective milling   B. progressive kiln drying
    C. finger jointed stock   D. scarf jointed stock

26. Of the following, the practice that is NOT used in wood finishing is the application of   26._____

    A. lacquer over varnish
    B. varnish over shellac
    C. wood filler over water stain
    D. lacquer over sanding sealer

27. When using screws to fasten two pieces of wood together, there should be a clamping action and the screw should penetrate the second piece a distance to equal _____ the length of the screw.   27._____

    A. 1/3   B. 2/3   C. 1/2   D. 3/4

28. The MOST common grades of pumice used for woodwork finishing are   28._____

    A. CC and CCC   B. DD and DDD
    C. EE and EEE   D. FF and FFF

29. Of the following, the dimensions that will result in the formation of a right triangle are   29._____

    A. 3' x 4' x 6'   B. 4' x 5' x 9'
    C. 6' x 8' x 10'   D. 7' x 9' x 13'

30. The label on a box of wood screws reads as follows: 1 gross, 3/4" #8 - F.H.B. wood screws.
The abbreviation F.H.B. means flat head   30._____

    A. brass   B. bright steel
    C. blue   D. bronze

KEY (CORRECT ANSWERS)

1.	B		16.	C
2.	C		17.	A
3.	D		18.	B
4.	A		19.	D
5.	D		20.	D
6.	B		21.	B
7.	A		22.	D
8.	C		23.	B
9.	B		24.	C
10.	D		25.	C
11.	C		26.	A
12.	B		27.	B
13.	B		28.	D
14.	C		29.	C
15.	B		30.	B

TEST 3

DIRECTIONS: Each question or incomplete statement is followed by several suggested answers or completions. Select the one that BEST answers the question or completes the statement. *PRINT THE LETTER OF THE CORRECT ANSWER IN THE SPACE AT THE RIGHT.*

1. MOST branches originate at the   1._____

    A. pith   B. bark   C. heartwood   D. sapwood

2. Of the following, the INACCURATELY matched pair is _____ pts. per inch.   2._____

    A. rip saw - 5 to 8   B. crosscut saw - 16 to 20
    C. back saw - 16   D. coping saw - 15

3. The process of conditioning sandpaper to make it pliable and to prevent cracking is   3._____

    A. gritting   B. pulling   C. limbering   D. racking

4. The BEST saw listed here to use for fine work in joinery is the _____ saw.   4._____

    A. rip   B. back   C. compass   D. crosscut

5. The mortise-and-tenon joint used MOST extensively in cabinet making is the   5._____

    A. blind   B. through   C. haunched   D. open

6. The PRINCIPAL constituent of wood is   6._____

    A. lignin   B. cellulose   C. gum   D. tannen

7. The twist drill which will make the SMALLEST hole is the   7._____

    A. A   B. #48   C. 1/8"   D. #52

8. The LARGEST trees found growing in the United States are the   8._____

    A. pine   B. redwood   C. walnut   D. maple

9. Ripsaw teeth are sharpened at an angle of   9._____

    A. $45°$ B. $60°$
    C. $90°$ D. none of the above

10. All of the following are natural abrasives EXCEPT   10._____

    A. sandstone   B. flint
    C. pumice   D. silicon carbide

11. When a tree is girdled, the vital part which is severed, causing the death of the tree, is   11._____
the

    A. cambium layer   B. bark
    C. cortex   D. annual ring

12. Of the following solvents, the one recommended for varnish is   12._____

    A. kerosene   B. turpentine
    C. alcohol   D. lacquer thinner

13. Shingles are USUALLY cut from   13.____

    A. chestnut   B. cypress   C. redwood   D. red cedar

14. The wood screw MOST suited for attaching hardware is the _____ head.   14.____

    A. flat   B. round   C. oval   D. fillister

15. Plywood is ordered by   15.____

    A. square foot   B. board foot
    C. linear foot   D. weight

16. The glue that should be used in boat construction is   16.____

    A. liquid hide   B. casein
    C. plastic resin   D. white liquid resin

17. The size of the dowel generally used in joining 1" thickness stock is   17.____

    A. 1/4"   B. 3/8"   C. 1/2"   D. 9/16"

18. The plane used MOST in the woodworking shop is the   18.____

    A. block   B. smooth   C. jack   D. jointer

19. Two-thirds of all plywood is made of   19.____

    A. Douglas fir   B. walnut
    C. pine   D. birch

20. The MOST commonly used hinge is the _____ hinge.   20.____

    A. surface   B. chest   C. Soss   D. butt

21. The tool which is generally used to make a 3/16" hole for screws is the   21.____

    A. Forstner bit   B. auger bit
    C. drill bit   D. brad awl

22. The length of a 6d nail is   22.____

    A. 1"   B. 2"   C. 1 1/2"   D. 3"

23. In relation to the combined depth of the two holes of a dowel joint, the length of the dowel is   23.____

    A. the same size   B. 1/16" shorter
    C. 1/4" shorter   D. 1/8" shorter

24. The purpose of linseed oil in paint is to   24.____

    A. give covering power
    B. thin out the paint
    C. give adhesiveness and elasticity to coat of paint when dry
    D. dry paint quickly

25. The material MOST used for wire nails is

    A. low carbon Bessemer steel
    B. malleable iron
    C. tungsten steel
    D. cast iron

25.____

26. Excelsior for packing purposes is obtained MOSTLY from

    A. hemlock   B. basswood   C. pine   D. redwood

26.____

27. The term *kerf* refers to

    A. gullet angle   B. the number of teeth
    C. the set of the saw   D. the thickness of the saw

27.____

28. Of the following statements regarding sandpaper, the one that is INACCURATE is: It is

    A. a cutting tool
    B. used after the chiseling operation
    C. composed of grains of stone
    D. graded in size

28.____

29. The method used in cutting nearly all the veneers in the United States is

    A. rotary cutting   B. sawing
    C. slicing   D. quarter-sawing

29.____

30. The name applied to the diameter of a wood screw is

    A. root   B. gauge   C. core   D. length

30.____

KEY (CORRECT ANSWERS)

1.	A	16.	C
2.	B	17.	B
3.	C	18.	C
4.	B	19.	A
5.	A	20.	D
6.	B	21.	C
7.	D	22.	B
8.	B	23.	D
9.	C	24.	C
10.	D	25.	A
11.	A	26.	B
12.	B	27.	C
13.	D	28.	B
14.	C	29.	A
15.	A	30.	B

TEST 4

DIRECTIONS: Each question or incomplete statement is followed by several suggested answers or completions. Select the one that BEST answers the question or completes the statement. *PRINT THE LETTER OF THE CORRECT ANSWER IN THE SPACE AT THE RIGHT.*

1. Blunting the end of a nail results in   1.____

    A. decreased holding power
    B. increased holding power
    C. lessening the possibility of splitting
    D. making it easier to drive

2. In woodworking, a chevron is frequently used to   2.____

    A. permit panels to *float*
    B. fasten joints
    C. conceal plywood edges
    D. fasten plywood to furring strips

3. A rose countersink used for countersinking F.H. wood screws has an included angle of _____ degrees.   3.____

    A. 45   B. 60   C. 75   D. 82

4. A *wobble-washer* is a device used in the making of   4.____

    A. window screens   B. stiles of doors
    C. dado joints   D. tapered strips

5. The term *flitch*, as used in woodworking, refers to the   5.____

    A. log from which veneers are cut
    B. squared log before it is sawed into lumber
    C. lumber from which moulding is shaped
    D. pile of lumber stacked for air-drying

6. Because of the shortage of clear pine, finger-jointing is extensively used in the production of   6.____

    A. door jambs and mouldings
    B. panel doors
    C. flooring
    D. furniture

7. In the construction of bow staves for archery, the wood MOST commonly used because of its strength and elasticity is   7.____

    A. oak   B. lemonwood   C. fir   D. larch

8. The glue used in both boat building and the laminating industry because of its waterproof qualities is   8.____

    A. resorcinol   B. casein
    C. white polyvinyl   D. urea-resin

9. Air drying of lumber produces material with a moisture content of approximately   9. ___

    A. 30%   B. 25%   C. 12-15%   D. 10%

10. To determine the number of board feet in a piece of lumber, the framing square may be   10.____
used by referring to the _____ table.

    A. Essex   B. Hudson   C. rafter   D. engineers

11. A core print is used on a pattern to   11._____

    A. form a recess in the mold in order to support a dry sand core
    B. permit *coping-out*
    C. reduce the amount of molten metal needed
    D. facilitate the flow of metal

12. As a good general rule, the taper of the pin of a dovetail is in the ratio of _____ to 1.   12.____

    A. 4   B. 6   C. 7   D. 8

13. The term *open coat* refers to a   13.____

    A. type of abrasive paper
    B. type of interior finish
    C. type of exterior finish
    D. method of gluing end grain

14. The size of Forstner bits is specified in _____ of an inch.   14.____

    A. 1/8's   B. 1/16's   C. 1/32's   D. 1/64's

15. The length of a jack plane as used in shops is   15.____

    A. 10-12"   B. 14-15"   C. 16"   D. 16-18"

16. Rubbing varnish is so-called because it   16.____

    A. is rubbed on the wood, leaving a surface free of brush marks
    B. is rubbed over a wash coat of sealer
    C. can be used to withstand abrasion
    D. can be rubbed to produce a smooth surface

17. Expansion shields are used for fastening objects to _____ walls.   17._____

    A. wood   B. hollow tile
    C. masonry   D. plaster

18. The gumming line on a circular saw blade refers to the   18.____

    A. diameter of the saw   B. depth of the tooth gullets
    C. set of the teeth   D. rake of the teeth

19. Staging nails are used for   19.____

    A. temporary construction work   B. building boxes
    C. heavy timbers   D. light work

20. The sliding *T* bevel is used to   20.___

    A. lay out a mortise
    B. lay out and transfer angles
    C. adjust the bevel on a plane iron
    D. measure the teeth of a handsaw

21. The formation of an interior opening or cavity in a casting necessitates the use of a   21.___

    A. loose piece   B. chaplet
    C. core   D. hanging cope

22. Hammers are classified by the   22.___

    A. length of the handle
    B. weight and type of the head
    C. length of the claw
    D. type of the shank

23. The term *jointing a saw* means filing the _____ of the teeth.   23.___

    A. sides   B. face   C. tops   D. back

24. When whetting a chisel on an oil stone, oil is put on the stone to   24.___

    A. lubricate the stone
    B. prevent the chisel from getting hot
    C. prevent the pores of the stone from clogging up with particles of steel
    D. keep the stone cool

25. Slip stones are designed for honing   25.___

    A. chisels   B. saws
    C. plane irons   D. gouges

26. When constructing a pattern to produce a casting, the allowance made for the contraction of the metal in the mold is called   26.___

    A. finish   B. draft
    C. shrinkage   D. filleting

27. The angle formed between the frog and the sole of a smooth plane is _____ degrees.   27.___

    A. 28   B. 30   C. 45   D. 60

28. Marine plywood differs from exterior grade plywood in that the   28.___

    A. wood is generally different
    B. glue is different
    C. type of core is different
    D. layers (plies) must be free of defects and voids

29. The markings *B 60 M 5 V E* would MOST likely be found on   29.____

    A. a package of abrasive paper
    B. a package of crocus cloth
    C. a grinding wheel
    D. exterior plywood

30. In stair construction, the general rule to follow concerning the riser and tread is   30.____

    A. riser and tread should total 17" to 18"
    B. riser and tread should always be less than 17"
    C. governed by the number of risers
    D. governed by the number of risers and platforms

KEY (CORRECT ANSWERS)

1.	C	16.	D
2.	B	17.	C
3.	D	18.	B
4.	C	19.	A
5.	A	20.	B
6.	A	21.	C
7.	B	22.	B
8.	A	23.	C
9.	C	24.	C
10.	A	25.	D
11.	A	26.	C
12.	B	27.	C
13.	A	28.	D
14.	B	29.	C
15.	B	30.	A

EXAMINATION SECTION
TEST 1

DIRECTIONS: Each question or incomplete statement is followed by several suggested answers or completions. Select the one that BEST answers the question or completes the statement. *PRINT THE LETTER OF THE CORRECT ANSWER IN THE SPACE AT THE RIGHT.*

1. To frame out a stair well, you need headers,

    A. trimmers, tail beams, and bridal irons
    B. trimmers, tail beams, and jacks
    C. trimmers, jacks, and bridal irons
    D. jacks, tail beams, and bridal irons

1._____

2. If it takes about 30 1bs. of 8-penny nails to nail 1000 board feet of finish flooring, the number of pounds of nails needed for the flooring in a 12' x 14' room is MOST NEARLY

    A. 4   B. 4½   C. 5   D. 5½

2._____

3. In construction drawings, the arrangement of members in a door frame is MOST frequently shown in a(n)

    A. plan view   B. section
    C. elevation   D. front view

3._____

4. A hollow ground blade would USUALLY be used on a circular saw for

    A. smooth cutting   B. rough cross cutting
    C. cutting dados   D. cutting old flooring

4._____

5. When erecting a 2" x 4" stud partition, the size of nail that should be used to toe-nail the stud to the sole plate is a _____ -penny.

    A. six   B. eight   C. ten   D. twelve

5._____

6. A blade for use with a diamond-shaped arbor is MOST frequently found on a _____ saw.

    A. jig   B. portable circular
    C. band   D. sabre

6._____

7. The one of the following that is NOT a common type of wood joint is a

    A. chamfer   B. rabbet   C. dado   D. butt

7._____

8. To determine whether the edge of a board has been planed square, it is BEST to use a _____ square.

    A. parallel   B. try   C. rafter   D. *T*

8._____

9. To prevent splintering of wood when planing end grain, it is BEST to plane from

    A. one edge of the wood to the opposite edge, parallel to the longer edge
    B. one edge of the wood to the opposite edge, parallel to the shorter edge
    C. opposite edges of the wood to the center
    D. the center of the wood to opposite edges

9._____

10. The number of teeth per inch on a backsaw is MOST frequently   10._____

    A. 6   B. 10   C. 14   D. 18

11. The number stamped on the shank of an auger bit refers to the size of the bit in _____   11._____
of an inch.

    A. 64ths   B. 32nds   C. 16ths   D. 8ths

12. A line level is MOST frequently used with a   12._____

    A. plumb bob   B. piece of string
    C. transit   D. tape

13. A gouge differs from a wood chisel PRINCIPALLY in that the blade on the gouge is   13._____

    A. curved
    B. longer
    C. shorter
    D. set at an angle to the handle

14. The FIRST operation in properly sharpening a hand saw is   14._____

    A. shaping   B. jointing   C. filing   D. setting

15. A compass saw MOST closely resembles, in appearance, a _____ saw.   15._____

    A. dovetail   B. coping   C. turning   D. keyhole

16. The size of a claw hammer refers to the _____ of the _____.   16._____

    A. length; head   B. diameter; face
    C. length; handle   D. weight; head

17. The one of the following power tools that has two tables, one lower than the other, is a   17._____

    A. radial saw   B. jointer
    C. shaper   D. router

18. The one of the following types of nails that is MOST frequently used to anchor wood to   18._____
masonry is a

    A. cut-nail   B. brad   C. wire nail   D. spike

19. One of the distinguishing features of a carriage bolt is that   19._____

    A. the head has a slot so that it can be driven with a screwdriver
    B. part of the body of the bolt, next to the head, is of square cross-section
    C. the entire body of the bolt from tip to head is threaded
    D. the head is square so that it can be turned with a wrench

20. A dog on a woodworking vise is used in conjunction with a   20._____

    A. bar clamp   B. brace
    C. bench stop   D. back bar

21. The type of wood used for finish flooring in apartments is MOST frequently   21._____

    A. pine   B. fir   C. walnut   D. oak

22. Interior trim is MOST frequently made of   22.____

    A.   cedar   B.   pine   C.   hemlock   D.   cypress

23. A *check* in lumber is caused by   23.____

    A.   improper drying   B.   exposure to rain
    C.   too great a stress   D.   a fungus

24. A *kerf* is made by a   24.____

    A.   hammer   B.   saw   C.   chisel   D.   plane

25. The term *dressed and matched* means the same as   25.____

    A.   mortise and tenon   B.   miter and spline
    C.   dado and rabbet   D.   tongue and groove

26. When framing a door opening, the wedging allowance between the trimmer stud and the   26.____
side jamb is MOST frequently

    A.   1/8"   B.   1/2"   C.   1"   D.   1¼"

27. The purpose of bridging is to distribute the load   27.____

    A.   over a window   B.   to adjoining rafters
    C.   over a door   D.   to adjoining joists

28. A bird's mouth cut is USUALLY found on a   28.____

    A.   joist   B.   stud   C.   lintel   D.   rafter

29. The BEST tool to use in laying out the cuts on a rafter is a _____ square.   29.____

    A.   T   B.   try
    C.   combination   D.   framing

30. The MAIN purpose of flashing is to   30.____

    A.   reflect the sun's rays   B.   prevent leakage
    C.   insulate walls   D.   strengthen sheathing

31. The type of glue that MUST be heated before using is _____ glue.   31.____

    A.   animal   B.   casein   C.   resin   D.   contact

32. A *parting stop* is usually found   32.____

    A.   between the ceiling of one story and the floor directly above
    B.   between sash in a double hung window
    C.   as part of a door jamb in a swinging door
    D.   along the ridge in a hip roof

33. As applied to stair construction, a *carriage* is the same as a   33.____

    A.   riser   B.   tread   C.   stringer   D.   cleat

34. When laying out stairs, the product of the number of inches in the tread, exclusive of nosing, and the number of inches in the riser should be less than   34.____

    A. 60   B. 65   C. 70   D. 75

35. Both doors and windows have   35.____

    A. lock rails   B. mullions
    C. stiles   D. meeting rails

36. The chiseled out portion of a door to which the butt of a hinge is fitted is called a   36.____

    A. rabbet   B. gain   C. mortise   D. set-back

37. The one of the following tools that should be used to cut a rabbet on a curved piece of wood is a   37.____

    A. shaper   B. jointer
    C. circular saw   D. lathe

38. Assume that the rise between two floor levels is 9'0". It is required to construct a stair between these two floors with risers that have a maximum height of 7½".
The SMALLEST number of risers that will satisfy this requirement is   38.____

    A. 12   B. 13   C. 14   D. 15

39. Zinc coated nails are often used in preference to ordinary nails MAINLY because they are   39.____

    A. easier to drive   B. harder to pull out
    C. stronger   D. more weather resistant

40. Of the following, the quality of white ash that is MOST important is its   40.____

    A. light weight
    B. high resistance to shock
    C. curly grain
    D. strength when wet

41. The thickness of finished maple flooring is MOST frequently   41.____

    A. 3/8"   B. 1/2"   C. 25/32"   D. 15/16"

42. Nails driven into 3/4" plywood, as compared to similar nails driven into 3/4" solid lumber made of the same grade of wood, are   42.____

    A. harder to pull out
    B. easier to pull out
    C. just as difficult to pull out
    D. harder or easier to pull out, depending on the number of plies in the plywood

TEST 2

DIRECTIONS: Each question or incomplete statement is followed by several suggested answers or completions. Select the one that BEST answers the question or completes the statement. *PRINT THE LETTER OF THE CORRECT ANSWER IN THE SPACE AT THE RIGHT.*

1. Where floor joists rest on a masonry wall, they should have a minimum bearing of _____ inches.

    A. 3   B. 4   C. 5   D. 6

1.____

2. Expansion shields would be used to

    A. protect exterior corners of walls
    B. provide a base for plaster
    C. protect a ceiling over a boiler
    D. anchor an object to a brick wall

2.____

3. When framing a window for use with a spring balance such as a *unique balance*, the allowance for pulley pockets is USUALLY

    A. smaller than when a sash weight is used
    B. the same as when a sash weight is used
    C. greater than when a sash weight is used
    D. completely eliminated

3.____

4. Plywood used for sheathing is MOST frequently _____ thick.

    A. 1/4"   B. 5/16"   C. 3/8"   D. 1/2"

4.____

5. The BEST size hinge to use for an exterior door measuring 1 3/8" thick and 36" wide is

    A. 3' x 3"   B. 3" x 3½"   C. 3½" x 4"   D.   4" x 4"

5.____

6. The MOST frequent method of framing a 2" x 4" partition over a small window is to _____ over the window.

    A. add a steel lintel   B. truss the wall
    C. double the headers   D. use hangers

6.____

7. Batter boards are MOST frequently used to

    A. establish corners for new construction
    B. determine the pitch of rafters
    C. support concrete forms
    D. brace stud partitions

7.____

8. A steel square would MOST frequently be used to lay out

    A. stud lengths in a partition
    B. casings for a door
    C. treads and risers for a staircase
    D. cuts for a mortise and tenon joint

8.____

51

9. Pumice stone is VERY often used in   9.____

    A. finishing furniture   B. honing tools
    C. setting bolts   D. smoothing concrete

10. Hand screws are USUALLY used when   10.____

    A. hanging shelves from a hollow partition
    B. glueing two pieces of wood together
    C. connecting sheet metal to wood
    D. erecting plywood walls

11. The MAIN reason for *setting* the teeth on a saw is to   11.____

    A. prevent the saw from binding
    B. permit the saw to make an even cut
    C. allow the saw to cut across the grain as well as with the grain
    D. eliminate the possibility of the *saw jumping* out of the cut

12. Assume that a peaked roof, with a 1/4 pitch, has a run of 12 ft.   12.____
The rise is

    A. 3'   B. 4'   C. 5'   D. 6'

13. A dovetail saw MOST closely resembles a _____ saw.   13.____

    A. keyhole   B. compass   C. back   D. rip

14. The one of the following that is part of a window trim is a(n)   14.____

    A. astragal   B. apron   C. panel   D. butt

15. Ship lap boards are USUALLY used as   15.____

    A. sills   B. plates   C. fascia   D. shingles

16. A plow MOST NEARLY resembles a   16.____

    A. mortise   B. dado   C. miter   D. spline

17. The one of the following types of wood that has the MOST open grain is   17.____

    A. pine   B. maple   C. oak   D. birch

18. Wood is usually treated in a kiln for the purpose of   18.____

    A. fireproofing it
    B. seasoning it
    C. preserving the wood against dampness
    D. termite-proofing it

19. The wood MOST commonly used for shingles in the East is   19.____

    A. cypress   B. birch   C. cedar   D. spruce

20. Lag screws are USUALLY driven by using a   20.____

    A. wrench   B. screwdriver
    C. hammer   D. brace

21. The one of the following that should be used for the final smoothing of wood before applying lacquer is　　21.____

    A. #1/2 garnet paper   B. a fine wood rasp
    C. 000 steel wool   D. 80 grit emery cloth

22. The total number of board feet in 18 2x4's, each measuring 8 ft. long, is MOST NEARLY　　22.____

    A. 90   B. 92   C. 96   D. 100

23. A *fire cut* is NORMALLY made on　　23.____

    A. studs   B. joists   C. rafters   D. plates

24. A *nail set* is a　　24.____

    A. group of the same type of nails in different sizes
    B. group of different types of nails in the same size
    C. tool used to pull nails
    D. tool used to countersink nails

25. Auger bits are BEST sharpened by using a　　25.____

    A. grinding wheel   B. file
    C. slip stone   D. whetstone

26. Casing nails are MOST similar in appearance to _____ nails.　　26.____

    A. roofing   B. common
    C. finishing   D. cut

27. A water level can be made by using　　27.____

    A. two glass tubes and a rubber hose
    B. a mason's level and two eye sights
    C. a pitch board and a mason's level
    D. a pitch board and a rubber hose

28. The purpose of a vapor barrier is to　　28.____

    A. prevent rain from entering a building through the wall
    B. protect the exterior wall of a building from moisture already inside the building
    C. prevent condensation of water in a cellar
    D. protect a building from ground water

29. Narrow boards are better for floor boards than wide boards of the same grade of lumber PRINCIPALLY because the narrow boards　　29.____

    A. cost less
    B. are easier to lay
    C. are stronger
    D. have less tendency to warp

30. 1" x 6" subflooring is USUALLY applied diagonally to the joists rather than perpendicular to the joists PRINCIPALLY because subflooring applied diagonally　　30.____

    A. costs less   B. is easier to lay
    C. is stronger   D. warps less

31. A purlin USUALLY supports   31.____

    A. rafters   B. sheathing   C. joists   D. studs

32. Insulation board is MOST frequently used as   32.____

    A. sheathing   B. subflooring
    C. siding   D. scantling

33. The one of the following that is NOT a type of rafter is a   33.____

    A. hip   B. valley   C. jack   D. tail

34. Lath is USUALLY used as a base for   34.____

    A. roofing   B. plaster
    C. waterproofing   D. insulation

35. A cricket is USUALLY located   35.____

    A. at the base of a parapet wall
    B. over an exterior door
    C. between the sill and the foundation
    D. in a non-bearing partition

36. The term *gambrel* refers to a type of   36.____

    A. window   B. roof   C. door   D. floor

37. Wainscoting is part of the finish of   37.____

    A. floors   B. ceiling   C. walls   D. doors

38. *Construction Grade* lumber is LEAST frequently used for   38.____

    A. joists   B. rafters   C. studs   D. girders

39. A strip of board that is used to fasten several pieces of lumber together is called a   39.____

    A. band   B. bracket   C. girt   D. cleat

40. Building paper is MOST often used to   40.____

    A. waterproof foundations
    B. insulate walls
    C. deaden sound
    D. protect floors during painting

41. One of the MAIN reasons for using furring strips is to   41.____

    A. fire retard a stairwell
    B. support floor joists
    C. provide clearance around a chimney
    D. permit building a straight ceiling

42. A *built up* girder USUALLY refers to a girder that is   42._____

    A. supported on posts
    B. cut to size at the building
    C. braced in position to prevent twisting
    D. made up of several pieces of wood fastened together

Questions 43-45.

DIRECTIONS: Questions 43 through 45, inclusive, are to be answered in accordance with the following paragraph.

    Wherever a soil pipe has to be provided for in a partition, special care must be taken that the hubs do not project beyond the finish face of the plaster. Before framing a building, it is desirable to ascertain where the stacks are and to provide for them. Building regulations require the stacks to be of 4-inch cast-iron even in small dwellings. With a 4-inch stack, the hub is 6 1/8 inches in diameter and, therefore, 2 by 6 studs must be used. Special care should be taken that no plaster comes in contact with a soil pipe, for subsequent settlement may cause cracking.

43. As used in the paragraph above, *subsequent* means MOST NEARLY   43._____

    A. heavy   B. sudden   C. later   D. soon

44. According to the above paragraph, 4" cast-iron soil pipes are used because   44._____

    A. they will not project beyond the face of the plaster
    B. it is easier to plaster over 4" pipe
    C. they can be located easier
    D. they are required by law

45. According to the above paragraph, the reason plaster should NOT be in direct contact   45._____
with soil pipe is because

    A. the plaster will be damaged by moisture
    B. rust will bleed through the plaster
    C. of the possibility of cracks due to settlement
    D. it is harder to plaster over 4" pipe

Questions 46-50.

DIRECTIONS: Questions 46 through 50, inclusive, refer to the floor plan of the building shown on the following page.

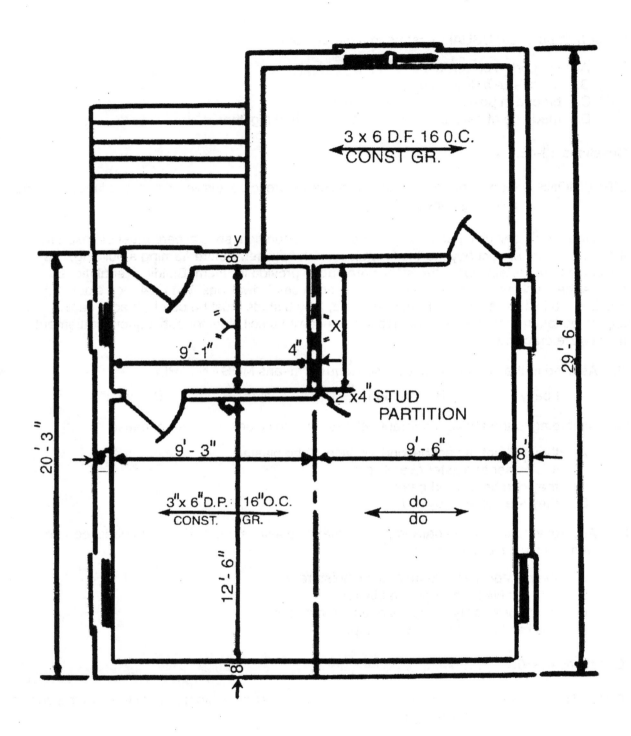

46. The dimension of the vestibule indicated by y is   46.____

    A. 6'0"   B. 6'1"   C. 6'2"   D. 6'3"

47. The number of risers indicated in the steps is   47.____

    A. 2   B. 3   C. 4   D. 5

48. The area of the large room, in square feet, is MOST NEARLY   48.____

    A. 292   B. 294   C. 296   D. 298

49. The letters D.F. over the arrow mean   49.____

    A. Douglas fir   B. diagonal subflooring
    C. doubled joists   D. deafening finish

50. If studs are placed a maximum of 16" on centers, the minimum number of studs required   50.____
in the section of wall marked X is

    A. 4   B. 5   C. 6   D. 7

KEY (CORRECT ANSWERS)

1.	B	11.	A	21.	C	31.	B	41.	D
2.	D	12.	D	22.	C	32.	A	42.	D
3.	D	13.	C	23.	B	33.	D	43.	C
4.	B	14.	B	24.	D	34.	B	44.	D
5.	D	15.	D	25.	B	35.	A	45.	C
6.	C	16.	B	26.	C	36.	B	46.	B
7.	A	17.	C	27.	A	37.	C	47.	D
8.	C	18.	B	28.	B	38.	C	48.	B
9.	A	19.	C	29.	D	39.	D	49.	A
10.	B	20.	A	30.	C	40.	B	50.	C

EXAMINATION SECTION
TEST 1

DIRECTIONS: Each question or incomplete statement is followed by several suggested answers or completions. Select the one that BEST answers the question or completes the statement. *PRINT THE LETTER OF THE CORRECT ANSWER IN THE SPACE AT THE RIGHT.*

1. The tool MOST frequently used to lay out a 45° angle on a piece of lumber is a   1.____

    A. combination square   B. try square
    C. marking gauge   D. divider

2. Beeswax would be MOST FREQUENTLY used on a(n)   2.____

    A. auger bit   B. scraper   C. hand saw   D. draw knife

3. A tool used to plane concave edges of furniture is a   3.____

    A. rabbet plane   B. wood scraper
    C. utility knife   D. spoke saw

4. A cap is found on a   4.____

    A. hammer   B. plane   C. power saw   D. lathe

5. The one of the following types of saw blades that is NOT commonly used on a circular saw is a   5.____

    A. dado   B. ply-tooth   C. novelty   D. tyler

6. The diameter of the arbor of a 12" circular saw is MOST LIKELY to be   6.____

    A. 3/8"   B. 1/2"   C. 5/8"   D. 3/4"

7. The one of the following woodworking operations that is NOT easily done on a drill press is   7.____

    A. routing   B. turning   C. shaping   D. mortising

8. A jointer may ALSO be used for   8.____

    A. mortising   B. routing   C. planing   D. shaping

9. The one of the following power tools that is NOT frequently built with a slot for a miter guage is a   9.____

    A. shaper   B. band saw   C. disc sander   D. radial saw

10. The abrasive grit on *sandpaper* is USUALLY   10.____

    A. pumice   B. boron   C. flint   D. talc

11. The abrasive grit on *open coat* paper for use on a power sander for woodwork is USUALLY   11.____

    A. tripoli   B. emery   C. aluminum oxide D. carborundum

12. The one of the following used in finishing furniture that has the FINEST grit is   12._____

    A. garnet   B. carborundum
    C. pumice   D. rottenstone

13. An expansive bit should be sharpened with a(n)   13._____

    A. auger bit file   B. mill file
    C. half round file   D. grinding wheel

14. The one of the following planes that is USUALLY used with one hand is the   14._____

    A. smoothing   B. block   C. jack   D. fore

15. When sharpening a hand saw, the FIRST operation is to file the teeth so that they are all   15._____
the same height.
This is known as

    A. shaping   B. setting   C. jointing   D. leveling

16. The tool that would be used to cut out a circular disc is a   16._____

    A. circular saw   B. shaper
    C. planer   D. band saw

17. A scale on which the inch graduations are divided into 12 subdivisions, each 1/12 of an   17._____
inch in length, is USUALLY found on a _____ square.

    A. try   B. combination
    C. rafter   D. T

18. The one of the following oils that is COMMONLY used for oilstones is   18._____

    A. penetrating   B. SAE #5
    C. vinsol   D. pike

19. A tool used in hanging doors is a   19._____

    A. butt gauge   B. reamer   C. C-clamp   D. trammel

20. A spur center is used on a   20._____

    A. jigsaw   B. drill press
    C. lathe   D. disc sander

21. The length of a certain screw is measured from the top of the head to the point.   21._____
The type of screw that this is MOST LIKELY to be is a

    A. round head   B. flat head   C. oval head   D. lag

22. The size of the drill that would be used to drill a body hole for a #7 wood screw is   22._____

    A. 3/32"   B. 5/32"   C. 7/32"   D. 9/32"

23. The one of the following types of bolts that would be used to anchor a shelf bracket to a   23._____
plywood partition is a

    A. carriage   B. expansion   C. drift   D. toggle

24. For ease in driving, screws are FREQUENTLY coated with   24.____

    A. casco   B. oil   C. soap   D. urea resins

25. The length of a 10-penny nail is   25.____

    A. 3"   B. 3 1/4"   C. 3 1/2"   D. 3 3/4"

26. To increase the holding power of nails, the nails are FREQUENTLY coated with   26.____

    A. alundum   B. aluminum   C. zinc   D. cement

27. Galvanized nails would MOST PROBABLY be used in nailing   27.____

    A. shingles   B. finished flooring
    C. joists   D. interior trim

28. Splitting of wood can be reduced by using nails with points that are   28.____

    A. long and sharp   B. blunt
    C. spirally grooved   D. common

29. The standard size of a 2" X 6" S4S is   29.____

    A. 1 5/8" X 5 5/8"   B. 1 5/8" X 5 3/4"
    C. 1 1/2" X 5 1/2"   D. 1 1/2" X 5 5/8"

30. The West Coast Lumber Inspection Bureau has recently changed the names of the   30.____
grades of lumber for Douglas Fir and Hemlock.
The grade that was PREVIOUSLY called No. 1 common is NOW called

    A. construction   B. utility
    C. select   D. structural

31. The strength of lumber is affected by   31.____

    A. whether it is cut from a live tree or a dead tree
    B. the time of the year in which the lumber is cut
    C. whether the tree is virgin growth or second growth
    D. the moisture content of the lumber

32. The one of the following woods that is classed as *open grained* is   32.____

    A. douglas fir   B. long leaf yellow pine
    C. spruce   D. oak

33. The one of the following woods that is classed as a hardwood is   33.____

    A. cedar   B. poplar
    C. douglas fir   D. hemlock

34. The one of the following woods that is MOST difficult to work with hand tools is   34.____

    A. cedar, northern white   B. pine, southern yellow
    C. hemlock, western   D. cypress, southern

35. The one of the following heartwoods that has the GREATEST resistance to decay is   35.____

    A. douglas fir   B. spruce   C. oak   D. birch

36. The one of the following woods that is EASIEST to glue is   36.____

     A. beech   B. birch   C. cedar   D. walnut

37. Flooring, for surfaces that will have very heavy wear, such as gymnasiums, is USUALLY made of   37.____

     A. oak   B. maple
     C. long leaf yellow pine   D. larch

38. The BEST grades of finished flooring are _____ sawed.   38.____

     A. quarter   B. flat   C. end   D. plain

39. Lumber used for floor joists in the East is USUALLY   39.____

     A. oak   B. gum   C. hemlock   D. pine

40. The wood MOST COMMONLY used for shingles is   40.____

     A. alder   B. larch   C. cedar   D. spruce

41. Millwork is USUALLY made of   41.____

     A. ash   B. chestnut   C. hemlock   D. pine

42. The wood MOST FREQUENTLY used for the rungs of the BEST quality ladders is   42.____

     A. locust   B. hickory   C. oak   D. balsam

43. Dressed and matched lumber would MOST LIKELY be   43.____

     A. dove-tailed   B. bevel siding
     C. crown molding   D. tongue and groove

44. Creosote is used to   44.____

     A. intensify the grain of wood prior to finishing
     B. preserve wood from rot
     C. glue wood in laminated girders
     D. prevent checking

45. The one of the following that is COMMONLY used as a vapor barrier is   45.____

     A. asphalt roll roofing   B. Kraft paper
     C. plywood   D. gypsum board

46. Corners of a building are USUALLY located by means of   46.____

     A. batter boards   B. framing squares
     C. line levels   D. base plates

47. Horizontal beams used to reinforce concrete forms and sheet piling are known as   47.____

     A. stirrups   B. walers   C. sheathing   D. braces

48. When using a post to shore a form for a reinforced concrete girder, the BEST practice is   48.____
to cut the post

    A.   to exact length, so that no driving will be required
    B.   slightly larger than required, so that the post must be driven into place
    C.   with a slight bevel, so that the post can be wedged into place
    D.   several inches too short, so that wedges will be needed

49. Corner posts of a frame building in the East MUST be at least the equivalent of three   49.____
_____ inch timbers.

    A. 2X4   B. 2X6   C. 3X6   D. 4X4

50. The size of cross bridging between joists is MOST FREQUENTLY   50.____

    A. 1" X 2"   B. 1" X 3"   C. 2" X 4"   D. 2" X 6"

KEY (CORRECT ANSWERS)

1.	A	11.	C	21.	B	31.	D	41.	D
2.	C	12.	D	22.	B	32.	D	42.	B
3.	D	13.	A	23.	D	33.	B	43.	D
4.	B	14.	B	24.	C	34.	B	44.	B
5.	D	15.	C	25.	A	35.	A	45.	A
6.	D	16.	D	26.	D	36.	C	46.	A
7.	B	17.	C	27.	A	37.	B	47.	B
8.	C	18.	D	28.	B	38.	A	48.	D
9.	D	19.	A	29.	A	39.	C	49.	A
10.	C	20.	C	30.	A	40.	C	50.	B

TEST 2

DIRECTIONS: Each question or incomplete statement is followed by several suggested answers or completions. Select the one that BEST answers the question or completes the statement. *PRINT THE LETTER OF THE CORRECT ANSWER IN THE SPACE AT THE RIGHT.*

1. The MAXIMUM spacing between bridging should be   1.____

   A. 6 ft.   B. 8 ft.   C. 10 ft.   D. 12 ft.

2. The one of the following methods of nailing cross bridging that is the MOST ACCEPT-   2.____
   ABLE is

   A. the tops and bottoms should be nailed before the subflooring is in place
   B. the tops and bottoms should be nailed after the subflooring is in place
   C. *only* the bottoms should be nailed. The tops should be nailed after the subflooring
       is in place
   D. *only* the tops should be nailed. The bottoms should be nailed after the subflooring
       is in place

3. The one of the following that may be used as a shim to raise the end of a joist resting on   3.____
   a concrete wall is

   A. gypsum block   B. wood
   C. sheet rock   D. slate

4. When framing joists around a chimney, the MINIMUM clear distance from wood to the   4.____
   chimney permitted in the East is

   A. 4"   B. 6"   C. 8"   D. 10"

5. The ends of joists are FREQUENTLY supported on   5.____

   A. hanger bolts   B. tie plates
   C. bridle irons   D. gusset plates

6. When there is a tight knot in a joist, the joist should   6.____

   A. be placed with the knot up
   B. be placed with the knot down
   C. be reinforced
   D. not be used

7. 7.____

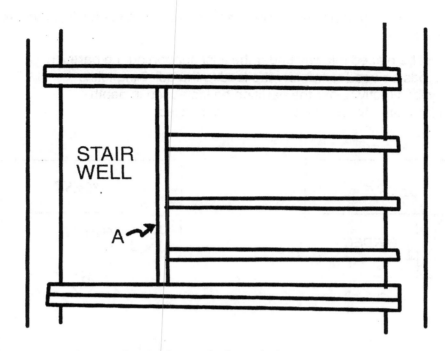

The short joist indicated by the letter *A* above is known as

A. trimmer   B. tail beam   C. header   D. lattice

8. 8.____

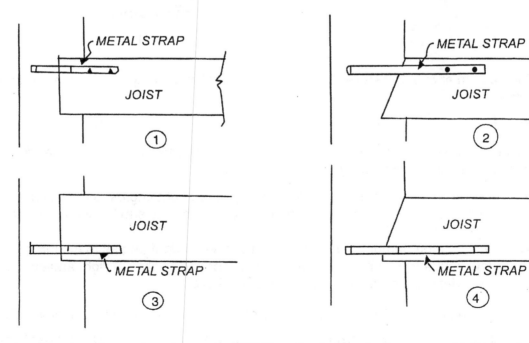

The diagram above that shows the BEST method of anchoring a wood joist to a brick is numbered

A. *1*   B. *2*   C. *3*   D. *4*

9. Where a non bearing partition runs over and is parallel to the joists, standard practice requires that   9.____

    A.   a post be placed midway under the joist supporting the partition
    B.   sag rods be used to transfer the load to the adjoining joists
    C.   the joist directly under the partition be increased in depth
    D.   the joist directly under the partition be doubled

10.   10.____

The diagram above that shows the BEST method of supporting a joist on a girder is numbered

    A.   *1*   B.   *2*   C.   *3*   D.   *4*

11. The one of the following statements that is CORRECT when *roofers* are used for sub-flooring is diagonal subflooring   11.____

    A.   requires less lumber than subflooring applied at right angles to the joists
    B.   requires approximately the same amount of lumber as subflooring applied at right angles to the joists
    C.   requires more lumber than subflooring applied at right angles to the joists
    D.   may require more or less lumber than subflooring applied at right angles to the joists, depending on the dimensions of the building

12. A timber laid directly on the ground or on a concrete base to support a floor is called a   12.____

    A.   sleeper   B.   sizing   C.   rail   D.   ledger board

13. Diagonal subflooring is preferred to subflooring laid square across the joists because the   13.____
diagonal subflooring

    A.   stiffens the building
    B.   is easier to lay
    C.   is more economical to lay
    D.   does not require as much nailing

14. A meeting rail is usually found on a   14.____

    A.   stair   B.   door   C.   roof   D.   window

15. The size of a sill plate, for a frame building, laid on a continuous concrete wall in the East   15.____
is USUALLY

    A.   4" X 6"   B.   4" X 10"   C.   2" X 10"   D.   2" X 8"

16. A valley is made watertight by means of a   16.____

    A.   cornice   B.   flashing   C.   drip sill   D.   furring

17. A strip of wood whose purpose is to assist the plasterers to make a straight wall is called   17.____
a

    A.   casing   B.   ground
    C.   belt course   D.   gauge

18. A hip rafter is framed between   18.____

    A.   plate and ridge   B.   plate and valley
    C.   valley and ridge   D.   valley and overhang

19. 2" X 8" rafters are being used on a roof with a pitch of one quarter.   19.____
The size of ridge board that would MOST PROBABLY be used is

    A.   2" X 8"   B.   3" X 8"   C.   2" X 10"   D.   2" X 12"

20. When planks intended to be used for roof rafters are not straight, the one of the following   20.____
statements that is CORRECT is

    A.   all rafters should be erected with the cambers (crown) up
    B.   all rafters should be erected with the cambers (crown) down
    C.   the rafters should be erected with the cambers (crown) alternately up and down
    D.   the plank should not be used for rafters

21.

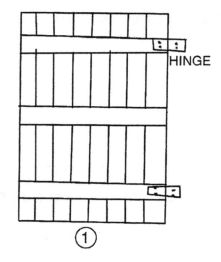

①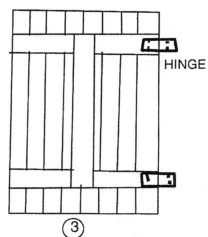

②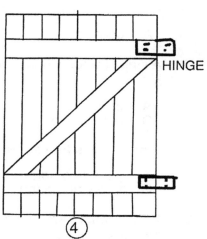

③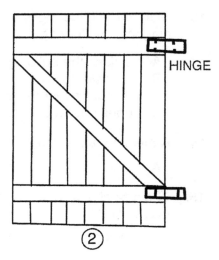

④

21._____

The diagram above that shows the BEST method of building a door for a shed is numbered

    A. *1*   *B.* *2*   C. *3*   D. *4*

22. A vertical member separating two windows is called a   22._____

    A. muntin   B. mullion   C. stile   D. casing

23. Wood girders framing on a masonry wall in the East should have a MINIMUM bearing of   23._____

    A. 2"   B. 4"   C. 6"   D. 8"

24. A collar beam is used to tie   24._____

    A. floor joists   B. laminated girders
    C. roof rafters   D. columns

25. Nosing would MOST probably be found in   25._____

    A. window frames   B. stairs
    C. saddles   D. scarfs

26. To help prevent plaster cracks when a 2" X 4" stud partition is cut for a doorway, it is   26.____
    USUAL to

    A.   provide a steel lintel B. use joint   B.   hangers
    C.   double the header   D.   corbel the studs

27. The side support for steps or stairs is called a   27.____

    A.   ledger board   B.   pitch board
    C.   riser   D.   stringer

28. The type of joint MOST FREQUENTLY used where baseboards meet at the corner of a   28.____
    room is a

    A.   miter   B.   mortise and tenon
    C.   spline   D.   butt

29. The purpose of a water table is to   29.____

    A.   prevent water from entering at the top of a foundation wall
    B.   distribute water from a downspout directly on the ground
    C.   prevent water from entering a cellar through the cellar floor
    D.   prevent water from leaking through a roof at the chimney

30. The one of the following materials that will produce the MOST rigid wall is _____   30.____
    sheathing.

    A.   1" X 8" horizontal
    B.   1" X 8" diagonal
    C.   29/32" fiberboard
    D.   1/4" plywood

31. Split ring connectors are COMMONLY used to   31.____

    A.   anchor joists to girders
    B.   join members of a truss
    C.   anchor veneer to framework
    D.   connect wood girder to steel column

32. A strike plate would be attached to a   32.____

    A.   sill   B.   fascia   C.   jamb   D.   saddle

33. Blanket insulation is USUALLY placed between   33.____

    A.   siding and sheathing
    B.   sheathing and vapor barrier
    C.   vapor barrier and rock lath
    D.   rock lath and finished plaster

34. A pipe column filled with concrete is called a   34.____

    A.   pintle   B.   buttress   C.   pilaster   D.   lally

35. If you were required to build forms for spandrels, the location of these forms would be at   35.____

     A. footing level between piers
     B. roof level between girders
     C. floor level between columns
     D. footing level over the grillage

36. Where a 2-inch horizontal hole must be made in a 3" X 12" floor joist supporting a uni-   36.____
form live load, the BEST place to make this hole is in the _____ of the joist at the
_____ of the span.

     A. center; end   B. bottom; end
     C. center; center   D. bottom; center

37. To strengthen box corners in new furniture, common practice is to use   37.____

     A. tie rods   B. molly bolts
     C. glue blocks   D. webbing

38. The joint MOST frequently used for attaching the sides of drawers to the fronts is   38.____

     A. mortise and tenon   B. doweled
     C. dovetailed   D. splined

39. The pitch of a roof is one-sixth. If the run is 10 ft., the rise is   39.____

     A. 1'-8"   B. 3'-4"   C. 5'-0"   D. 6'-8"

40. The number of board feet in a 3" X 8", 16 ft. long, is   40.____

     A. 26   B. 28   C. 30   D. 32

41. A right triangle has sides of 5, 12, and 13 inches respectively.   41.____
The area of the triangle, is, in square inches,

     A. 30   B. 32 1/2   C. 60   D. 78

42. The one of the following that would be the dimension used to lay out a right angle is   42.____
_____ feet.

     A. 3, 4, 6   B. 4, 5, 9   C. 6, 8, 10   D. 7, 9, 13

43. A partition wall, with no openings in it, is to be 46 ft. long.   43.____
If studs are spaced 16" o.c. maximum, the number of studs that should be used in this
wall is

     A. 33   B. 34   C. 35   D. 36

44. A flight of stairs has 8 risers. The number of treads it has is   44.____

     A. 7   B. 8   C. 9   D. 10

45. A round post 4 inches in diameter and 4 feet high can carry 12,000 pounds.   45.____
A 6-inch post of the same height, and the same grade and species of wood, can carry
_____ pounds.

     A. 18,000   B. 21,000   C. 24,000   D. 27,000

46. The sum of the following dimensions,
4'-3 1/4", 3'-2 15/16", 2'-3 1/2", 3'-4 3/4", 4'-7 3/16" is

    A.   17'-9 7/16"   B.   17'-9 1/2"
    C.   17'-9 9/16"   D.   17'-9 5/8"

46.____

Questions 47 - 50.

    Questions 47 to 50 refer to the sketch below representing the 1st floor plan of a small tool shed.

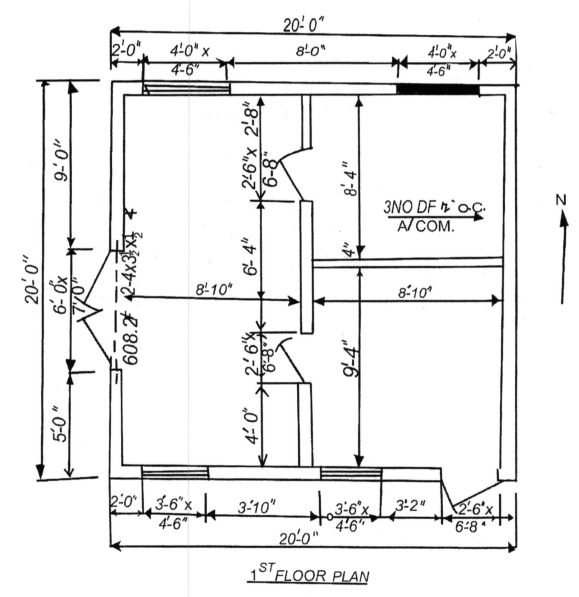

1ST FLOOR PLAN

47. The width* of the windows in the south wall of the building is

    A. 2'-6"   B. 3'-6"   C. 3'-10"   D. 4'-6"

47.____

48. The lintel over the large doorway is a

    A. single wood girder   B. built up wood girder
    C. steel beam and plates   D. steel channel and angles

49. The size of the LARGEST room is

    A. 8'-10" X 16'-0"   B. 8'-10" X 17'-0"
    C. 8'-10" X 18'-0"   D. 8'-10" X 19'-0"

50. The floor area of the SMALLEST room is, in square feet, MOST NEARLY

    A. 72   B. 74   C. 76   D. 78

KEY (CORRECT ANSWERS)

1.	B	11.	C	21.	B	31.	B	41.	A
2.	D	12.	A	22.	B	32.	C	42.	C
3.	D	13.	A	23.	B	33.	B	43.	D
4.	A	14.	D	24.	C	34.	D	44.	A
5.	C	15.	A	25.	B	35.	C	45.	D
6.	A	16.	B	26.	C	36.	C	46.	D
7.	C	17.	B	27.	D	37.	C	47.	B
8.	D	18.	A	28.	D	38.	C	48.	D
9.	D	19.	C	29.	A	39.	B	49.	C
10.	A	20.	A	30.	D	40.	D	50.	B

CARPENTRY

EXAMINATION SECTION
TEST 1

DIRECTIONS: Each question or incomplete statement is followed by several suggested answers or completions. Select the one that BEST answers the question or completes the statement. *PRINT THE LETTER OF THE CORRECT ANSWER IN THE SPACE AT THE RIGHT.*

1. In a ratchet bit brace, the part that holds the bit is called the   1.____

   A. vise   B. chuck   C. pawl   D. cam ring

2. The BEST tool to use as a guide when scribing a line perpendicular to the side of a 2" x 4" stud is a   2.____

   A. T-square   B. Try square
   C. Batter board   D. Parallel bar

3. Of the following planes, the *one* that does NOT have a double plane iron is the   3.____

   A. block plane   B. jack plane
   C. fore plane   D. smooth plane

4. Of the following files, the BEST one to use to sharpen a rip-saw is a   4.____

   A. taper   B. flat bastard   C. mill   D. half round

5. The size of auger bit to select in order to bore a 5/8" hole is   5.____

   A. #5   B. #8   C. #10   D. #12

6. The type of circular saw used for cutting grooves that are *wider* than the cut that can be made by ordinary saws is known as a   6.____

   A. dado set   B. rabbet set
   C. scarf set   D. dove tail set

7. Of the following saws, the *one* that should be used for cutting circular disks out of 5/8" plywood is a   7.____

   A. circular saw   B. buck saw
   C. back saw   D. band saw

8. The saw used in a miter box is a   8.____

   A. compass saw   B. coping saw
   C. back saw   D. hacksaw

9. Of the following, the BEST wood to use for the handle of a claw hammer is   9.____

   A. pine   B. hickory   C. cypress   D. elm

10. A 3" belt sander requires a 3 x 21 belt. The "21" refers to the belt's   10.____

    A. grit number   B. diameter
    C. contact area   D. length

11. In sharpening a paring chisel, a carpenter should grind the bevel at an angle of, *approximately,*   11.____

    A. 5°   B. 15°   C. 25°   D. 35°

12. "Dressing" a saw has to do with   12.____

    A. lowering the height of the teeth
    B. removing burrs from the side of the teeth
    C. lowering of the tooth gullets
    D. tilting the file upward at the end of the stroke

13. To cut a 1/4-inch chamfer in a piece of wood two feet long, a carpenter should use a   13.____

    A. chisel   B. plane   C. saw   D. hone

14. To tighten a lag screw, a Carpenter should use a   14.____

    A. mallet   B. Phillips head screw-driver
    C. wrench   D. hammer

15. When boring a hole through a thin piece of wood, the bit that will LEAST splinter the backside of the wood is a(n)   15.____

    A. center bit   B. expensive bit
    C. Foerstner bit   D. countersink bit

16. Shown below is a sketch of a hinge.   16.____

The hinge is a(n)

    A. T-hinge   B. strap hinge
    C. piano hinge   D. offset hinge

17. A hinged strap with a slotted flap that passes over a staple and is secured by a padlock is known as a   17.____

    A. hasp   B. hamper   C. harbinger   D. hawk

18. To bend saw teeth to the proper angle, a carpenter should use a   18.____

    A. saw screed   B. saw tap   C. saw bit   D. saw set

19. A tool used to make a pilot hole for starting a screw in wood is a(n)   19.____

    A. grommet   B. cotter pin   C. awl   D. counter point

20. The tool to use to finish driving a nail into corners and moldings is a nail   20.____

    A. set   B. punch   C. pin   D. all

21. Of the following fasteners, the *one* that is LEAST often used in structural wood work is a   21.____

    A. lag screw   B. wood screw   C. nail   D. spike

22. When wood loses moisture, it shrinks in   22.____

    A. thickness and width and expands in length
    B. thickness and expands in width and length
    C. width and length and expands in thickness
    D. thickness, width, and length

23. Of the following types of commercial nails, the *one* that has the GREATEST withdrawal resistance is a   23.____

    A. cement-coated nail   B. galvanized nail
    C. chemically etched nail   D. spirally grooved nail

24. The grit number for a 1/0 sand paper is   24.____

    A. 200   B. 100   C. 80   D. 60

25. The length of a 6d nail is   25.____

    A. 1 3/4"   B. 2"   C. 2 1/4"   D. 2 3/4"

KEYS (CORRECT ANSWERS)

1.	B		11.	B
2.	B		12.	B
3.	A		13.	B
4.	A		14.	C
5.	C		15.	A
6.	A		16.	D
7.	D		17.	A
8.	C		18.	D
9.	B		19.	C
10.	D		20.	A

21.	B
22.	D
23.	D
24.	C
25.	B

TEST 2

Each question or incomplete statement is followed by several suggested answers or completions. Select the one that BEST answers the question or completes the statement. *PRINT THE LETTER OF THE CORRECT ANSWER IN THE SPACE AT THE RIGHT.*

1. The number of board feet in 15 pieces of lumber 2" x 10" by 12 feet long is   1._____

   A. 30   B. 300   C. 600   D. 900

2. When unpainted wood is left outdoors for a considerable time, the color of the wood *usually* changes to   2._____

   A. brown   B. gray   C. yellow   D. amber

3. When wood is to be in permanent contact with earth, it should be treated with   3._____

   A. creosote   B. tri-sodium phosphate
   C. sodium chloride   D. sal ammoniac

4. A panic bolt is *most frequently* installed on a   4._____

   A. window   B. door   C. roof scuttle   D. skylight

5. Of the following, the BEST reason for oiling plywood concrete forms is to   5._____

   A. lubricate the concrete during vibration
   B. allow forms to be removed easily
   C. decrease porosity of the plywood
   D. prevent seapage of rain water into the concrete in case it rains while the concrete is setting

6. Of the following species of wood, the *one* that is classified as a SOFT wood is   6._____

   A. chestnut   B. white ash   C. birch   D. cypress

7. S.S. glass means   7._____

   A. Smooth Surface glass   B. Silicone Surface glass
   C. Single Strength glass   D. Square Sides glass

8. Of the following types of wood, the *one* that is NOT coarsegrained is   8._____

   A. oak   B. pine   C. walnut   D. chestnut

9. The one of the following materials that does NOT contain wood is   9._____

   A. hardboard   B. compressed board
   C. particle board   D. masonite

10. Plywood sub flooring is used instead of 1" x 6" sub flooring MAINLY because it   10._____

   A. is more sound proof   B. is easier to install
   C. is more fire resistant   D. makes the floor more rigid

11. Wainscoting paneling would be installed on a   11._____

   A. wall   B. floor   C. ceiling   D. roof

12. According to the building code, galvanized wire staple fasteners in plywood may   12._____

    A. not be used anywhere in buildings
    B. be used on roofs only
    C. be used on wall sheathing only
    D. be used on roofs and wall sheathing

13. Galvanized nails are nails that are coated with   13._____

    A. brass   B. cadmium   C. copper   D. zinc

14. The tip of a Phillips screwdriver is   14._____

    A. elliptical   B. pointed   C. flat   D. concave

15. Putlogs are used PRIMARILY on   15._____

    A. ladders   B. scaffolds   C. horses   D. hatchways

16. The tapered end of a file that fits into a wood handle is called the   16._____

    A. tip   B. heel   C. edge   D. tang

17. Of the following bolts, the type which has a *round* head is the   17._____

    A. machine bolt   B. stud bolt
    C. carriage bolt   D. coupling bolt

18. A metal T-anchor would be used on a   18._____

    A. door   B. window   C. joist   D. stud

19. A lock that is surface mounted on the side of a door is known as a   19._____

    A. rim lock   B. tenon lock
    C. mortise lock   D. flange lock

20. Clapboards are *generally* used for   20._____

    A. stair treads   B. wood siding
    C. window sills   D. roof copings

21. Shown below is a sketch of the floor joists in a building.   21._____

ELEVATION

The pieces of wood marked X are known as

    A. bridging   B. bracketing   C. corbeling   D. casing

22. A specification for a belt sander states that it is *UL* approved. The *UL* in the specification is an abbreviation of   22.____

    A. Universal Listing   B. Underwriters Laboratories
    C. Unlimited Liability   D. Use Limited

23. Shown below is a sketch of a wood joint.   23.____

PLAN

ELEVATION

The wood joint is a

    A. peg tenon   B. plain dovetail butt
    C. dovetail half lap   D. blind housed tenon

Questions 24-25.

DIRECTIONS: Questions 24 and 25 refer to the wood form work for concrete shown in the sketch at the top of the next page.

24. The horizontal member X is known as a   24.____

    A. girt   B. soldier   C. pivot   D. waler

25. The horizontal member Y is known as a   25.____

    A. scab   B. ledger   C. kerf   D. putlog

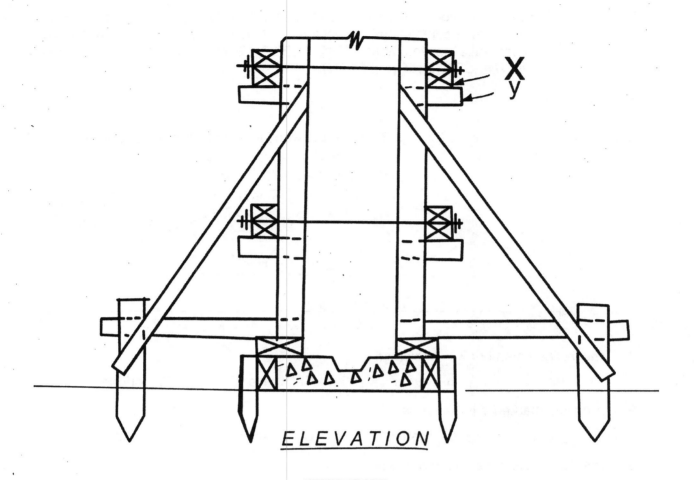

ELEVATION

KEYS (CORRECT ANSWERS)

1.	B		11.	A
2.	B		12.	D
3.	A		13.	D
4.	B		14.	B
5.	B		15.	B
6.	D		16.	D
7.	C		17.	C
8.	B		18.	C
9.	B		19.	A
10.	B		20.	B

21.	A
22.	B
23.	A
24.	D
25.	B

TEST 3

DIRECTIONS: Each question or incomplete statement is followed by several suggested answers or completions. Select the one that BEST answers the question or completes the statement. *PRINT THE LETTER OF THE CORRECT ANSWER IN THE SPACE AT THE RIGHT.*

Questions 1-3.

DIRECTIONS: Questions 1 through 3 refer to the wood truss shown in the sketch below.

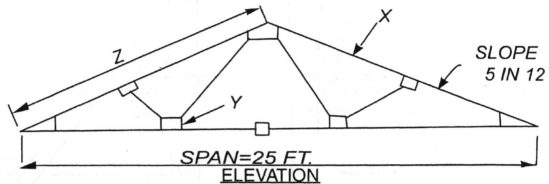

1. The inclined member X is known as a   1.____

   A. ridge   B. rafter   C. brace   D. bridge

2. The plate marked Y is known as a(n)   2.____

   A. gusset   B. batten   C. spacer   D. anchor

3. The TOTAL distance Z is, *most nearly,*   3.____

   A. 13' 2 1/2"   B. 13' 4 1/2"
   C. 13' 6 1/2"   D. 13' 8 1/2"

4. Shown in the sketch below is a bolted timber.   4.____

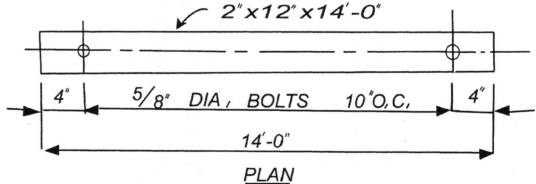

The number of 5/8" diameter bolts required is

   A. 15   B. 16   C. 17   D. 18

5. Plywood sub flooring 5/8" thick has a Panel Identification Index of 42/20. The "20" indicates the

    A. maximum allowable load in pounds on a square foot of panel
    B. maximum permitted center to center distance in inches between floor joists
    C. weight of a cubic foot of panel
    D. minimum number of 8d nails required per panel

5.____

6. An identifying symbol *HDO* G-1 - DFPA - 19 - PS1 - 66 is stamped on the edge of a plywood panel. The *HDO* part of this code stands for

    A. Heavy Duty Outside
    B. High Density Oak
    C. High Density Overlaid
    D. Housing Development Organization

6.____

7. Floor plans showing the modification of partitions are drawn to a scale of 1/4" to a foot. If the length of a partition shown on the drawing scales 6 3/8", then the ACTUAL length of the partition would be, *most nearly,*

    A. 2.4' 6"   B. 25' 2"   C. 24' 4"   D. 25' 6"

7.____

Questions 8-9.

DIRECTIONS: Questions 8 and 9 refer to the DETAIL shown below.

8. The number of 3/8" bolts in the roof scuttle is

    A. 6   B. 8   C. 10   D. 12

8.____

9. In the DETAIL shown above, the number of 2" x 6" planks required is

    A. 7   B. 8   C. 9   D. 10

9.____

10. On an alteration drawing, the location of *new* partitions would be shown on a(n)

    A. floor plan   B. front elevation
    C. frame cross-section   D. end view

10.____

11. A drawing specifies "3-1x6-*Fas* - Wh. Oak S4S." *Fas* is an abbreviation for

    A. face all sides   B. finish all sides
    C. fabricate as specified   D. firsts and seconds

11.____

12.

In the trade mark shown above, the abbreviation DFPA means

   A. Designers Fabricated Partition Authority
   B. Douglas Fir Plywood Association
   C. Developed Fabricated Plyscord Association
   D. Durable Federal Product Authority

12.____

13. A specification calls for *3/8" x 2"* steel lag screw. In the above specification, the *3/8"* refers to the

   A. height of the head
   B. root diameter of the thread
   C. diameter of the body under the head
   D. length of body under the head

13.____

14. The following statement is taken from a specification scope of work:
    Except as otherwise specified, furnish, deliver and install all carpentry and millwork, related work and equipment as required by the drawings and specified herein, including, but not necessarily limited to the following:
    All rough carpentry work where shown on the drawings, implied as necessary, specified, or otherwise required including permanent and temporary grounds, blocking, rough framing and *bucks,* nailing strips, furring, plates, under floor sleepers, and the like.
In the above passage, *bucks* would refer to

   A. doors   B. windows   C. scuppers   D. hatchways

14.____

15. A specification states the floowing:
    Blind nail T and G flooring.
In the above specification, the word *blind* means to

   A. bend   B. hide   C. extrude   D. offset

15.____

16. Narrow strips of wood nailed upon walls and ceilings as a support for the wall or ceiling finish is known as

   A. darbying   B. batting   C. heading   D. furring

16.____

17. A purlin is *most similar* in function to a

   A. stud   B. jamb   C. joist   D. batten

17.____

18. If the riser for a stairway is 7 1/2" high, then the *number* of risers required for a flight of stairs 8' 9" high is

   A. 11   B. 12   C. 13   D. 14

18.____

19. The one of the following that is NOT a common type of wood joint is the 19.____

    A. scarf   B. dovetail   C. chamfer   D. butt

20. A flat hardwood board set on the floor in a doorway between rooms is called a 20.____

    A. mullion   B. jamb   C. jib   D. saddle

21. Shown below is a section of wall and flooring of a building. 21.____

FINISHED WALL

BASE BOARD

FINISHED FLOOR

X

In the drawing shown above, the molding X represents a

    A. base mold   B. shoe mold   C. bed mold   D. lip mold

22. Shown below is a section through a door. 22.____

INSIDE

DOOR

WALL   WALL

OUTSIDE

The hand of the door is

    A. left hand regular   B. left hand reverse
    C. right hand regular   D. right hand reverse

23. A 3/4" thick flooring is to be laid directly on joists. 23.____
Of the following, the BEST practice is to nail the flooring to

    A. every joist
    B. every third joist
    C. end joists only
    D. end joists and middle joist only

24. The margin which should be left all around between the edges of an 8" x 10" pane of   24.____
glass and the sides of the rabbet in a wood sash is

    A. none   B. 1/16"   C. 3/16"   D. 5/16"

25. The *horizontal* wood member which supports the load over a window or door is known as   25.____
a

    A. putlog   B. ledger   C. collar   D. lintel

————

KEYS (CORRECT ANSWERS)

1.	B		11.	D
2.	A		12.	B
3.	C		13.	C
4.	C		14.	A
5.	B		15.	B
6.	C		16.	D
7.	D		17.	C
8.	D		18.	D
9.	D		19.	C
10.	A		20.	D

21.	B
22.	A
23.	A
24.	B
25.	D

————

TEST 4

DIRECTIONS: Each question or incomplete statement is followed by several suggested answers or completions. Select the one that BEST answers the question or completes the statement. *PRINT THE LETTER OF THE CORRECT ANSWER IN THE SPACE AT THE RIGHT.*

1. Shown below is a section of a wood joint.   1.____

ELEVATION

The joint shown is a

   A.   dove tail joint   B.   double butt joint
   C.   shiplap joint   D.   serrated joint

2. In the construction of a wood frame building a metal shield is sometimes placed between   2.____
the top of concrete piers and the wood girder resting on it. Of the following, the BEST
reason for the metal shield is to

   A.   spread the load over the pier
   B.   protect the wood against termites
   C.   insulate the building
   D.   allow for expansion and contraction of the wood

3. Shown below is a section of wood molding.   3.____

The molding is a(n)

   A.   reed   B.   center bead   C.   round   D.   astragal

4. Wood is *most frequently* fastened to a concrete wall by a(n)   4.____

   A.   clevis   B.   expansion shield
   C.   brad   D.   spike

5. A bolt with a spring loaded part used for securing wood to a hollow wall is a(n)   5.____

   A.   anchor bolt   B.   stud bolt
   C.   toggle bolt   D.   toe bolt

6. The *number* of plane surfaces in a gambrel roof is   6.____

   A.   two   B.   three   C.   four   D.   five

7. The *vertical* members of a wooden door are known as

    A. rails   B. stiles   C. struts   D. sleepers

7.____

8. Driving nails at an angle to the surface of a vertical member in order to get adequate penetration into a horizontal member is known as

    A. clinch nailing   B. toe nailing
    C. French nailing   D. dog nailing

8.____

9. Collar beams are *most often* used on

    A. trusses   B. windows   C. girders   D. doors

9.____

10. On a double-hung wood window, the stool rests on the sill *and* a(n)

    A. mullion   B. rail   C. apron   D. stud

10.____

11. In a two-story wood frame building, a fascia would be found on the

    A. roof   B. stair   C. wall   D. floor

11.____

12. A baluster is a part of a

    A. roof   B. wall   C. door   D. stair

12.____

13. Stair treads rest on strips of wood nailed to the inside of stair stringers. These strips of wood are called

    A. shims   B. wedges   C. stubs   D. cleats

13.____

14. Shown at the top of the next page is a section through the exterior wall of a building. The member X represents a

    A. wall plate   B. ledger
    C. fire stop   D. girder

14.____

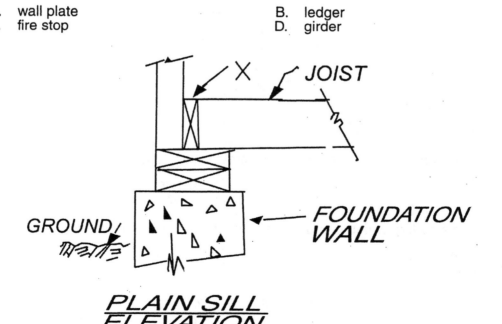

X   JOIST

GROUND

FOUNDATION WALL

PLAIN SILL ELEVATION

15. The molded projection which finishes the top of the wall of a building is a   15.____

    A. coronet   B. corolla   C. cornice   D. cupola

16. The BEST reason for *not* painting a wood ladder is that   16.____

    A. the paint may conceal cracks
    B. it saves money not to paint the ladder
    C. painted ladder rungs get very slippery when wet
    D. the wood used is difficult to paint and paint spalls readily

17. In case of a fire in the floor below in a building in which a carpenter is making alterations,   17.____
the BEST action for the carpenter to take is to

    A. walk quickly to the nearest stairway
    B. walk quickly to the nearest elevator
    C. collect all his tools and run to the nearest stairway
    D. open all the windows and run to the nearest stairway

18. Of the following, the one that should NOT be used as an improvised tourniquet is a   18.____

    A. leather belt   B. Venetian blind cord
    C. stocking   D. scarf

19. Of the following character traits, the BEST trait for a supervisor to have is   19.____

    A. optimism   B. rudeness   C. punctuality   D. decisiveness

20. Assume that you are acting in charge of a group of carpenters in the field installing parti-   20.____
tions. You receive a telephone call from the office that they need a carpenter in the shop
to do a rush job.
Of the following, the BEST action to take is to

    A. send the senior carpenter
    B. send the most capable carpenter
    C. ask for volunteers
    D. send the least capable carpenter

21. In assigning additional work to carpenters, a supervisor should FIRST consider the car-   21.____
penter's

    A. seniority   B. previous output
    C. current work load   D. attendance record

22. In checking the daily work of several carpenters at different locations, a good supervisor   22.____
should visit the men

    A. according to each man's seniority
    B. at random hours each day
    C. according to location of nearest man first and farthest man last
    D. according to priority of when jobs have to be completed

23. Of the following jobs, the *one* that usually requires WRITTEN orders instead of ORAL orders is a job where   23.____

    A. progress can be easily checked
    B. emergency exists
    C. a mistake will be of little consequence
    D. many details are involved

24. To obtain cooperation from subordinates, a supervisor should   24.____

    A. complain about it   B. practice it
    C. demand it   D. suggest it

25. The BEST way to *temporarily* store oily sawdust in a carpenter shop before discarding   25.____
    the sawdust is in a

    A. metal can with a perforated metal cover
    B. metal can without a cover
    C. metal can with an air-tight metal cover
    D. perforated metal can with an air-tight cover

————

KEYS (CORRECT ANSWERS)

1.	C	11.	A
2.	B	12.	D
3.	D	13.	D
4.	B	14.	C
5.	C	15.	C
6.	C	16.	A
7.	B	17.	A
8.	B	18.	B
9.	A	19.	D
10.	C	20.	B

21.	C
22.	B
23.	D
24.	B
25.	C

————

TEST 5

DIRECTIONS: For questions 1 through 11, the item referred to is shown to the right of the question.

1. The bolt shown should be used
   A. in foundations
   B. in cement curbs
   C. to connect rails
   D. to connect girders

1.____

2. The screw shown is called a
   A. set screw
   B. anchor screw
   C. lag screw
   D. toggle screw

2.____

3. The anchor shown should be used in a
   A. wood post
   B. concrete wall
   C. plaster wall
   D. gypsum block wall

3.____

4. The wrench shown is called a(n)
   A. monkey wrench
   B. Allen wrench
   C. "L" wrench
   D. socket wrench

4.____

5. The anchor shown should be used in a
   A. concrete wall
   B. veneer wall
   C. plaster wall
   D. brick wall

5.____

6. The cutter shown should be used on
   A. pipes
   B. cables
   C. re-bars
   D. bolts

6.____

7. The saw shown is called a
   A. coping saw
   B. cross-cut saw
   C. hack saw
   D. back saw

7.____

8. The tool shown is a
   A. "D" clamp
   B. "C" clamp
   C. pipe vise
   D. metal vise

8.____

9. The tool shown is a
   A. hawk
   B. trowel
   C. screed
   D. joiner

9.____

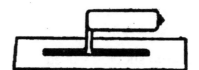

10. The tool shown is called a
   A. try square
   B. T-bevel
   C. miter box
   D. miter square

10.____

11. The tool shown should be used to
   A. make grooves in side walks
   B. turn lead bends
   C. make copper bends
   D. finish brick joints

11.____

_____

KEYS (CORRECT ANSWERS)

1.	A	6.	A
2.	C	7.	D
3.	B	8.	B
4.	B	9.	B
5.	C	10.	C
		11.	A

_____

GLOSSARY OF CARPENTRY AND BUILDING CONSTRUCTION TERMS

TABLE OF CONTENTS

GLOSSARY OF CARPENTY AND BUILDING CONSTRUCTION TERMS

Anchor - Irons of special form used to fasten together timbers or masonry.

Anchor bolts - Bolt which fastens columns, girders, or other members to concrete or masonry.

Backing - The bevel on the top edge of a hip rafter that allows the roofing board to fit the top of the rafter without leaving a triangular space between it and the lower side of the roof covering.

Balloon frame - The lightest and most economical form of construction, in which the studding and corner posts are set up in continuous lengths from first-floor line or sill to the roof plate.

Baluster - A small pillar or column used to support a rail.

Balustrade - A series of balusters connected by a rail, generally used for porches, balconies, and the like.

Band - A low, flat molding.

Base - The bottom of a column; the finish of a room at the junction of the walls and floor.

Batten (cleat) - A narrow strip of board used to fasten several pieces together.

Batter board - A temporary framework used to assist in locating the corners when laying a foundation.

Batter pile - Pile driven at an angle to brace a structure against lateral thrust.

Beam - An inclusive term for joists, girders, rafters, and purlins.

Bedding - A filling of mortar, putty, or other substance in order to secure a firm bearing.

Belt course - A horizontal board across or around a building, usually made of a flat member and a molding.

Bent -A single vertical framework consisting of horizontal and vertical members supporting the deck of a bridge or pier.

Bevel board (pitch board) - A board used in framing a roof or stairway to lay out bevels.

Board - Lumber less than 2 inches thick.

Board foot - The equivalent of a board 1 foot square and 1 inch thick.

Boarding in - The process of nailing boards on the outside studding of a house.

Bollard - Steel or cast iron post to which large ships are tied.

Braces - Pieces fitted and firmly fastened to two others at any angle in order to strengthen the angle thus treated.

Bracket - A projecting support for a shelf or other structure.

Break joints - To arrange joints so that they do not come directly under or over the joints of adjoining pieces, as in shingling, siding, etc.

Bridging - Pieces fitted in pairs from the bottom of one floor joist to the top of adjacent joists, and crossed to distribute the floor load; sometimes pieces of width equal to the joists and fitted neatly between them.

Building paper - Cheap, thick paper, used to insulate a building before the siding or roofing is put on; sometimes placed between double floors.

Built-up member - A single structural component made from several pieces fastened together.

Built-up timber - A timber made of several pieces fastened together, and forming one of larger dimension.

Carriages - The supports or the steps and risers of a flight of stairs.

Casement - A window in which the sash opens upon hinges.

Casing - The trimming around a door or window opening, either outside or inside, or the finished lumber around a post or beam, etc.

Ceiling - Narrow, matched boards; sheathing of the surfaces that inclose the upper side of room.

Center-hung sash - A sash hung on its centers so that it swings on a horizontal axis.

Chamfer - A beveled surface cut upon the corner of a piece of wood.

Checks - Splits or cracks in a board, ordinarily caused by seasoning.

Chock - Heavy timber fitted between fender piles along wheel guard of a pier or wharf.

Chord - The principal member of a truss on either the top or bottom.

Clamp - A mechanical device used to hold two or more pieces together.

Clapboards - A special form of outside covering of a house; siding.

Cleats - Metal arms extending horizontally from a relatively low base used for securing small ships, tugs, and work boats.

Column - A square, rectangular, or cylindrical support for roofs, ceilings, and so forth, composed of base, shaft, and capital.

Combination frame - A combination of the principal features of the full and balloon frames.

Concrete - An artificial building material made by mixing cement and sand with gravel, broken stone, or other aggregate, and sufficient water to cause the cement to set and bind the entire mass.

Conductors - Pipes for conducting water from a roof to the ground or to a receptacle or drain; downspout.

Cornice - The molded projection which finishes the top of the wall of a building.

Counterflashings - Strips of metal used to prevent water from entering the top edge of the vertical side of a roof flashing; they also allow expansion and contraction without danger of breaking the flashing.

Cross brace - Bracing with two intersecting diagonals.

Deadening - Construction intended to prevent the passage of sound.

Decking - Heavy plank floor of a pier or bridge.

Diagonal - Inclined member of a truss or bracing system used for stiffening and wind bracing.

Drip - The projection of a window sill or water table to allow the water to drain clear of the side of the house below it.

Fascia - A flat member of a cornice or other finish, generally the board of the cornice to whic the gutter is fastened.

Fender pile - Outside row of piles that protects a pier or wharf from damage by ships.

Fitter - Piece used to fill space between two surfaces.

Flashing - The material used and the process of making watertight the roof intersections and other exposed places on the outside of the house.

Flue - The opening in a chimney through which smoke passes.

Flush - Adjacent surfaces even, or in same plane (with reference to two structural pieces).

Footing - An enlargement at the lower end of a wall, pier, or column, to distribute the load.

Footing form - A wooden or steel structure, placed around the footing that will hold the concrete to the desired shape and size.

Foundation - That part of a building or wall which supports the superstructure.

Frame - The surrounding or inclosing woodwork of windows, doors, etc., and the timber skeleton of building.

Framing - The rough timber structure of a building, including interior and exterior walls, floor, roof, and ceilings.

Full frame - The old fashioned mortised-and-tenoned frame, in which every joint was mortised and tenoned. Rarely used at the present time.

Furring - Narrow strips of board nailed upon the walls and ceilings to form a straight surface upon which to lay the laths or other finish.

Gable - The vertical triangular end of a building from the eaves to the apex of the roof.

Gage - A tool used by carpenters to strike a line parallel to the edge of a board.

Gambrel - A symmetrical roof with two different pitches or slopes on each side.

Girder - A timber used to support wall beams or joists.

Girt (ribband) - The horizontal member of the walls of a full or combination frame house which supports the floor joists or is flush with the top of the joists.

Grade - The horizontal ground level of a building or structure.

Groove - A long hollow channel cut by a tool, into which a piece fits or in which it works. Two special types of grooves are the *dado,* a rectangular groove cut across the full width of a piece, and the *housing,* a groove cut at any angle with the grain and part way across a piece. Dados are used in sliding doors, window frames, etc.; housings are used for framing stair risers and threads in a string.

Ground - A strip of wood assisting the plasterer in making a straight wall and in giving a place to which the finish of the room may be nailed.

Hanger - Vertical-tension member supporting a load.

Header - A short joist into which the common joists are framed around or over an opening.

Headroom - The clear space between floor line and ceiling, as in a stairway.

Heel of a rafter - The end or foot that rests on the wall plate.

Hip roof - A roof which slopes up toward the center from all sides, necessitating a hip rafter at each corner.

Jack rafter - A short rafter framing between the wall plate; a hip rafter.

Jamb - The side piece or post of an opening; sometimes applied to the door frame.

Joint-butt - Squared ends or ends and edges adjoining each other:

    Dovetail - Joint made by cutting pins the shape of dovetails which fit between dovetail upon another piece.

    Drawboard - A mortise-and-tenon joint with holes so bored that when a pin is driven through, the joint becomes tighter.

    Fished - An end butt splice strengthened by pieces nailed on the sides.

    Glue - A joint held together with glue.

    Halved - A joint made by cutting half the wood away from each piece so as to bring the sides flush.

    Housed - A joint in which a piece is grooved to receive the piece which is to form the other part of the joint.

    Lap - A joint of two pieces lapping over each other.

    Mortised - A joint made by cutting a hole or mortise, in one piece, and a tenon, or piece to fit the hole, upon the other.

    Rub - A flue joint made by carefully fitting the edges together, spreading glue between them, and rubbing the pieces back and forth until the pieces are well rubbed together.

    Scarfed - A timber spliced by cutting various shapes of shoulders, or jogs, which fit each other.

Joists - Timbers supporting the floorboards.

Kerf - The cut made by a saw.

Knee brace - A corner brace, fastened at an angle from wall stud to rafter, stiffening a wood or steel frame to prevent angular movement.

Laths - Narrow strips to support plastering.

Lattice - Crossed wood, iron plate, or bars.

Ledgerboard - The support for the second-floor joists of a balloon-frame house, or for similar uses; ribband.

Level - A term describing the position of a line or plane when parallel to the surface of still water; an instrument or tool used in testing for horizontal and vertical surfaces, and in determining differences of elevation.

*Lintel (cap -)*A horizontal structural member spanning an opening, and supporting a wall load.

Lookout - The end of a rafter, or the construction which projects beyond the sides of a house to support the eaves; also the projecting timbers at the gables which support the verge boards.

Louver - A kind of window, generally in peaks of gables and the tops of towers, provided with horizontal slots which exclude rain and snow and allow ventilation.

Lumber - Sawed parts of a log such as boards, planks, scantling, and timber.

Matching, or tonguing and grooving - The method used in cutting the edges of a board to make a tongue on one edge and a groove on the other.

Meeting rail - The bottom rail of the upper sash of a double-hung window. Sometimes called the check-rail.

Member - A single piece in a structure, complete in itself.

Miter - The joint formed by two abutting pieces meeting at an angle.

Molding Base - The molding on the top of a baseboard.

> *Bed* – A molding used to cover the joint between the plancier and frieze (horizontal decorative band around the wall of a room); also used as a base molding upon heavy work, and sometimes as a member of a cornice.

> *Lip* - A molding with a lip which overlaps the piece against which the back of the molding rests.

> *Picture* - A molding shaped to form a support for picture hooks, often placed at some distance from the ceiling upon the wall to form the lower edge of the frieze.

> *Rake* - The cornice upon the gable edge of a pitch roof, the members of which are made to fit those of the molding of the horizontal eaves.

Mortise - The hole which is to receive a tenon, or any hole cut into or through a piece by a chisel; generally of rectangular shape.

Mullion - The construction between the openings of a window frame to accommodate two or more windows.

Muntin - The vertical member between two panels of the same piece of panel work. The vertical sash-bars separating the different panels of glass.

Newel - The principal post of the foot of a staircase; also the central support of a winding flight of stairs.

Nosing - The part of a stair tread which projects over the riser, or any similar projection; a term applied to the rounded edge of a board.

Pad eyes - Metal rings mounted vertically on a plate for tying small vessels.

Partition - A permanent interior wall which serves to divide a building into rooms.

Pier-(a) Timber, concrete, or masonry supports for girders, posts, or arches. (b) Intermediate supports for adjacent ends of two bridge spans. (c) Structure extending outward from shore into water used as a dock for ships.

*Piers-*Masonry supports, set independently of the main foundation.

Pilaster - A portion of a square column, usually set within or against a wall.

Piles - Long posts driven into the soil in swampy locations or whenever it is difficult to secure a firm foundation, upon which the footing course of masonry or other timbers are laid.

Piling - Large timbers or poles driven into the ground or the bed of a stream to make a firm foundation.

Pitch - Inclination or slope, as for roofs or stairs, or the rise divided by the span.

Pitch board - A board sawed to the exact shape formed by the stair tread, riser, and slope of the stairs and used to lay out the carriage and stringers.

Plan - A horizontal geometrical section of a building, showing the walls, doors, windows, stairs, chimneys, columns, etc.

Plank - A wide piece of sawed timber, usually 1 1/2 to 4 1/2 inches thick and 6 inches or more wide.

Plaster - A mixture of lime, hair, and sand, or of lime, cement, and sand, used to cover outside and inside wall surfaces.

Plate - The top horizontal piece of the walls of a frame building upon which the roof rests.

Plate cut - The cut in a rafter which rests upon the plate; sometimes called the seat cut.

Plow - To cut a groove running in the same direction as the grain of the wood.

Plumb cut - Any cut made in a vertical plane; the vertical cut at the top end of a rafter.

Ply - A term used to denote a layer or thickness of building or roofing paper as two-ply, three-ply, etc.

Porch - An ornamental entrance way.

Post - A timber set on end to support a wall, girder, or other member of the structure.

Pulley stile - The member of a window frame which contains the pulleys and between which the edges of the sash slide.

Purlin - A timber supporting several rafters at one or more points, or the roof sheeting directly.

Rabbet or rebate - A corner cut out of an edge of a piece of wood.

Rafter - The beams that slope from the ridge of a roof to the eaves and make up the main body of the roof's framework.

Rafters, common - Those which run square with the plate and extend to the ridge.

    Cripple - Those which cut between valley and hip rafters.

    Hip - Those extending from the outside angle of the plates toward the apex of the roof.

    Jacks - Those square with the plate and intersecting the hip rafter.

    Valley - Those extending from an inside angle of the plates toward the ridge or center line of the house.

Rail - The horizontal members of a balustrade or panel work.

Rake - The trim of a building extending in an oblique line, as rake dado or molding.

Return - The continuation of a molding or finish of any kind in a different direction.

Ribband - (See Ledgerboard.)

Ridge - The top edge or corner formed by the intersection of two roof surfaces.

Ridge cut - (See Plumb cut.)

Rise - The vertical distance through which anything rises, as the rise of a roof or stair.

Riser - The vertical board between two treads of a flight of stairs.

Roofing - The material put on a roof to make it wind and waterproof.

Rubble - Roughly broken quarry stone.

Rubble masonry - Uncut stone, used for rough work, foundations, backing, and the like.

Run - The length of the horizontal projection of a piece such as a rafter when in position.

Saddle board - The finish of the ridge of a pitch-roof house. Sometimes called comb board.

Sash - The framework which holds the glass in a window.

Sawing, plain - Lumber sawed regardless of the grain, the log simply squared and sawed to the desired thickness; sometimes called slash or bastard sawed.

Scab - A short piece of lumber used to splice, or to prevent movement of two other pieces.

Scaffold or staging - A temporary structure or platform enabling workmen to reach high places.

Scale - A short measurement used as a proportionate part of a larger dimension. The scale of a drawing is expressed as 14 inch = 1 foot.

Scantling - Lumber with a cross-section ranging from 2 by 4 inches to 4 by 4 inches.

Scarfing - A joint between two pieces of wood which allows them to be spliced lengthwise.

Scotia - A hollow molding used as a part of a cornice, and often under the nosing of a stair tread.

Scribing - The marking of a piece of wood to provide for the fitting of one of its surfaces to the irregular surface of another.

Seat cut or plate cut - The cut at the bottom end of a rafter to allow it to fit upon the plate.

Seat of a rafter - The horizontal cut upon the bottom end of a rafter which rests upon the top of the plate.

Section - A drawing showing the kind, arrangement, and proportions of the various parts of a structure. It is assumed that the structure is cut by a plane, and the section is the view gained by looking in one direction.

Shakes - Imperfections in timber caused during the growth of the timber by high winds or imperfect conditions of growth.

Sheathing - Wall boards, roofing boards; generally applied to narrow boards laid with a space between them, according to the length of a shingle exposed to weather.

Sheathing paper - The paper used under siding or shingles to insulate in the house; building papers.

Siding - The outside finish between the casings.

Sills - The horizontal timbers of a house which either rest upon the masonry foundations or, in the absence of such, form the foundations.

Sizing - Working material to the desired size; a coating of glue, shellac, or other substance applied to a surface to prepare it for painting or other method of finish.

Sleeper - A timber laid on the ground to support a floor joist.

Span - The distance between the bearings of a timber or arch.

Specifications - The written or printed directions regarding the details of a building or other construction.

Splice - Joining of two similar members in a straight line.

Square - A tool used by mechanics to obtain accuracy; a term applied to a surface including 100 square feet.

Stairs, box - Those built between walls, and usually with no support except the wall.

Standing finish - Term applied to the finish of the openings and the base, and all other finish work necessary for the inside.

Stringer - A long horizontal timber in a structure supporting a floor.

Stucco - A fine plaster used for interior decoration and fine work; also for rough outside wall coverings.

Stud - An upright beam in the framework of a building.

Studding - The framework of a partition or the wall of a house; usually referred to as 2 by 4@s.

Sub floor - A wood floor which is laid over the floor joists and on which the finished floor is laid.

Threshold - The beveled piece over which the door swings; sometimes called a carpet strip.

Tie beam (collar beam) - A beam so situated that it ties the principal rafters of a roof together and prevents them from thrusting the plate out of line.

Timber - Lumber with cross-section over 4 by 6 inches, such as posts, sills, and girders.

Tin shingle - A small piece of tin used in flashing and repairing a shingle roof.

Top plate - Piece of lumber supporting ends of rafters.

To the iveather - A term applied to the projecting of shingles or siding beyond the course above.

Tread - The horizontal part of a step.

Trim - A term sometimes applied to outside or interior finished woodwork and the finish around openings.

Trimmer - The beam or floor joist into which a header is framed.

Trimming - Putting the inside and outside finish and hardware upon a building.

Truss - Structural framework of triangular units for supporting loads over long spans.

Valleys - The internal angle formed by the two slopes of a roof.

Verge boards - The boards which serve as the eaves finish on the gable end of a building.

Vestibule - An entrance to a house; usually inclosed.

Wainscoting - Matched boarding or panel work covering the lower portion of a wall.

Wale - A horizontal beam.

Wash - The slant upon a sill, capping, etc., to allow the water to run off easily.

Water table - The finish at the bottom of a house which carries water away from the foundation.

Wharf - A structure that provides berthing space for vessels, to facilitate loading and discharge of cargo.

Wind ("i" pronounced as in "kind") - A term used to describe the surface of a board when twisted (winding) or when resting upon two diagonally opposite corners, if laid upon a perfectly flat surface.

Wooden brick - Piece of seasoned wood, made the size of a brick, and laid where it is necessary to provide a nailing space in masonry walls.

ABBREVIATIONS AND SYMBOLS
CONTENTS

Page

ABBREVIATIONS AND SYMBOLS

1. Abbreviations

The following abbreviations in connection with lumber are used by the carpenter:

```
AD - - - - - - - - -air-dried
al - - - - - - - - - -all length
av - - - - - - - - - -average
avw - - - - - - - -average width
avl - - - - - - - - -average length
bd - - - - - - - - -board
bd ft - - - - - - -board foot
bdl- - - - - - - - -bundle
bev - - - - - - - -beveled
bm - - - - - - - -board (foot) measure
btr - - - - - - - - -better
clg- - - - - - - - -ceiling
clr - - - - - - - - -clear
CM - - - - - - - -center matched; that is, tongue-and-groove joints are made along the center of
                   the edge of the piece
Com - - - - - - -common
Csg- - - - - - - -casing
Ctg - - - - - - - -crating
cu ft- - - - - - - -cubic foot
D & CM - - - - -dressed (one or two sides) and center matched
D & M - - - - - -dressed and matched; that is, dressed one or two sides and tongue and
                  grooved on the edges. The match may be center or standard
DS - - - - - - - -drop siding
D & SM - - - - -dressed (one or two sides) and standard matched
D 2S & CM- - - -dressed two sides and center matched
D 2S & M- - - -dressed two sides and (center of standard) matched
D 2S & SM- - - -dressed two sides and standard matched
Dim - - - - - - -dimension
E- - - - - - - - - -edge
FAS- - - - - - - -firsts and seconds, a combined grade of the two upper grades of hardwoods
fbk- - - - - - - - -flat back
fcty - - - - - - - -factory (lumber)
FG - - - - - - - -flat grain
Flg - - - - - - - -flooring
fok- - - - - - - - -free of knots
Frm - - - - - - -framing
ft - - - - - - - - - -foot or feet
Hdl - - - - - - - -handle (stock)
Hdwd- - - - - - -hardwood
Hrt - - - - - - - -heart
Hrtwd - - - - - -heartwood
in - - - - - - - - - -inch or inches
```

```
KD ---------kiln-dried
kd ---------knocked down
lbr ---------lumber
lgr ---------longer
lgth --------length
linft --------linear foot, that is, 12 inches
LR---------log run
Lr MCO ------log run, mill culls out
M ---------thousand
MFBM -------thousand (feet) board measure
MCO --------mill culls out
Merch ------merchantable
MR ---------mill run
msm -------thousand (feet) surface measure
mw --------mixed width
No---------number
1s & 2s ------ones and twos, a combined grade of the hardwood grades of firsts and sec-
                onds
Ord --------order
P-----------planed
Pat --------pattern
Pky --------picky
Pln --------plain, as in plain sawed
Pn---------partition
Qtd --------quartered (with reference to hardwoods)
rd ---------round
rdm -------random
res --------resawed
rf g --------roofing
Rfrs--------roofers
rip --------ripped
rl ---------random length
rw ---------random width
S & E ------surfaced one side and one edge
S2S & M -----surfaced two sides and standard or center matched
S2S & SM ----.surfaced two sides and standard matched
Sap -------sapwood
S1E -------surfaced one edge
S1S1E -----surf aced one side and one edge
S1S2E -----surfaced one side and two edges
S2E -------surfaced two edges
S4S --------.surfaced four sides
S & CM -----surfaced one or two sides and center matched
S & M ------surfaced and matched; that is, surfaced one or two sides and tongued and
                grooved on the edges. The match may be center or standard.
S & SM -----surfaced one or two sides and standard matched
S2S & CM ----surfaced two sides and center matched
Sap -------sapwood
SB --------standard bead
Sd---------seasoned
```

Sdg - - - - - - - -siding
Sel - - - - - - - - -select
SESd- - - - - - - -square-edge siding
sf - - - - - - - - - -surface foot; that is, an area of 1 square foot
Stfwd- - - - - - -softwood
ShD - - - - - - - -shipping dry
Ship - - - - - - - -shiplap
Sm - - - - - - - - -standard matched
sm - - - - - - - - -surface measure
snd - - - - - - - - -sap no defect
snd - - - - - - - - -sound
sq - - - - - - - - - -square
sq E - - - - - - - -square edge
sq E & S - - - - -square edge and sound
sqrs- - - - - - - -squares
Std - - - - - - - - -standard
stk- - - - - - - - - -stock
SW - - - - - - - - -sound wormy
T & G - - - - - - -tongued and grooved
TB & S - - - - - -top, bottom, and sides
tbrs - - - - - - - -timbers
VG - - - - - - - - -vertical grain
wal - - - - - - - - -wider, all length
wdr - - - - - - - -wider
wt - - - - - - - - - -weight
wth - - - - - - - -width

2. Symbols

Symbols commonly used in carpentry are given below. For additional information on the various symbols used in construction plans and blueprints, refer to TM 5-704.

    a. *Architectural*

Tile -

Earth -

Plaster -

Sheet metal -

Built-in cabinet -

Outside door: Brick wall - - - - - - - - - - - - - - - - -

                    Frame wall - - - - - - - - - - - - - - - -

Inside door: Frame wall - - - - - - - - - - - - - - - - - -

Brick -

Firebrick -

Concrete -

Cast concrete block -

Insulation : Loose fill -

                Board or quilts - - - - - - - - - - - - - - - - -

Cut stone -

Ashlar -

Shingles (siding) -

Wood, rough -

Wood, finished -

Cased or arched openings - - - - - - - - - - - - - - - - -

Single caseinent window - - - - - - - - - - - - - - - - - -

Double hung windows -

Double casement window - - - - - - - - - - - - - - - - - -

b. *Plumbing*

Bathtubs:

Corner - - - - - - - - - -

Free standing - - - - - -

Floor drain- - - - - - - - - -

Shower drain - - - - - - - -

Hot-water tank- - - - - - - ⃝ н.w.т.

Grease trap - - - - - - - - -

Hose bibb or sill cock - - -

Lavatories:

Pedestal - - - - - - - - -

Wall-hung - - - - - - - - -

Corner. - - - - - - - - - -

Toilets:

Tank - - - - - - - - - - - -

Flush valve - - - - - - - -

Urinals:

Stall-type - - - - - - - - -

Wall-hung. - - - - - - - -

Laundry trays - - - - - -

Built-in shower - - - - -

Shower - - - - - - - - - - -

Sinks:

Single drain board.

Double drain board.

C. *Electrical*

Pull switch - - - - - - - - - ●⃝ₚₛ   Ceiling outlet - - - - - - - ⊕

Single-pole switch - - - - - S₁   Wall bracket - - - - - - - ⊸⊕

Single convenience out-
Double-pole switch - - - - - S₂   let - - - - - - - - - - - - - ⊨⊖

Double convenience out-
Triple-pole switch - - - - - - S₃   let - - - - - - - - - - - - - ⊨⊖₂

Ceiling outlet. gas & elec-
Buzzer - - - - - - - - - - - - ⌐□   tric - - - - - - - - - - - - - ⬥

Floor outlet - - - - - - - - - ⊕   Motor - - - - - - - - - - - ⓒ

Bell - - - - - - - - - - - - - - ◖□   Light outlet with wir-   ⊕
                                         ing and switches indi-
Drop cord - - - - - - - - - - ⊚   cated - - - - - - - - - - -

CPSIA information can be obtained
at www.ICGtesting.com
Printed in the USA
LVHW022051171219
640814LV00022B/543